A GARDENER'S GUIDE TO

CLIMATE
ADAPTIVE
GARDENING

A GARDENER'S GUIDE TO

CLIMATE ADAPTIVE GARDENING

The essential guide to gardening sustainably

KELVIN MASON

THE CROWOOD PRESS

First published in 2023 by
The Crowood Press Ltd
Ramsbury, Marlborough
Wiltshire SN8 2HR

enquiries@crowood.com

www.crowood.com

British Library Cataloguing-in-Publication Data
A catalogue record for this book is available from the British Library.

ISBN 978 0 7198 4269 6

Cover design by Blue Sunflower Creative

All photographs are the author's, with the exception of pages 48 and 60, which are Wikimedia Commons.

Typeset by Envisage IT
Printed and bound in India by Thomson Press India Ltd

CONTENTS

INTRODUCTION

To start, we should consider what climate change actually is and how likely it is to affect our gardens, landscapes and plants, as well as how we grow them. Climate change is not new; it has been gradually building up over the last century. It is now at the point where it is causing problems and we have enough knowledge to know that things are only going to get worse in the future unless we do something about it.

WHAT IS CLIMATE CHANGE?

Climate change is a very gradual change in our climate over many years, resulting in alterations to the weather patterns in various parts of the world. Although, at first, the changes do not look too untoward, many of them are detrimental to our way of living and are causing environmental problems such as drought, flooding, storms and heavy rainfall. These are problems that have occurred in recent years and are predicted to get worse in the future, leaving a generation with many large-scale issues to solve, including possible mass extinction of some species, increased damage to property and the environment, and larger weather extremes.

The effects of climate change are caused by the gradual rise in global temperature caused by increasing levels of carbon dioxide (CO_2) and other greenhouse gases, such as methane and nitrous oxide, in the atmosphere. These gases accumulate in the upper atmosphere and trap heat from the sun within the earth's atmosphere, slowly raising the temperature. At the time of writing, the world is approximately 1.2°C warmer than pre-industrial levels of the nineteenth century. In that time the CO_2 levels have risen by approximately 50 per cent to nearly 400ppm.

These changes have been caused by mankind and most of them have happened in the last fifty years owing to the use of fossil fuels to provide energy for electricity, heating, manufacturing and transport. To prevent the worse consequences of climate change occurring, we need to limit the rise in global temperatures to 1.5°C by the end of this century. As things are at present, the temperature is predicted to rise to 2.4°C by 2100 – some scientists are even predicting a rise of at least 4°C, which would have massive consequences to the planet, its environment and its plants and animals.

The weather of the early 2000s and recent catastrophes will just be a forewarning of what is likely to come by the end of the century. Taking 2021 as an example, there was extensive flooding in parts of Europe and China, storms in the tropics (even in the UK), hurricanes and typhoons in the USA, as well as large wildfires in Australia, Greece, Canada and the US. Some farmland is turning into desert owing to droughts, heatwaves and soil erosion caused by poor or no soil care.

HOW CAN WE SLOW DOWN OR STOP CLIMATE CHANGE?

To try to prevent climate change from happening we all need to take some action, and the aim of this book is to offer guidance on what can be done in the garden to adapt to these changes and still grow good-quality plants and food. One single thing or person is not going to solve climate change – it will need many actions by many people – but we can all do our bit and make a difference. Many small actions, such as living a more sustainable life, growing more of your food, reducing your carbon footprint and encouraging others to do the same, will make a difference over time.

It is up to the politicians to lead and set strategies and targets, and we need to do what we can to meet these targets. It will take a bit of effort and we will need to change our lifestyles a little but the alternative for future generations does not bear thinking about. We owe it to them to leave a planet that is in a condition suitable for living on.

If a few people plant a tree it will make little difference, but if everyone in the UK (approximately 66 million at the last count) plants a tree, this starts to make a bigger difference. Over time, they will sequester carbon from the atmosphere, reduce pollution, provide shade and reduce windspeed. Sequestering carbon into trees will not solve climate change on its own, but it *will* help, and tree planting should be encouraged. There are trees suitable for every garden (even small ones), it is just a case of choosing the right plant for the right place. We can all do more than plant a tree, as I hope this book will show.

If we all do nothing, or very little, the likely effects on the UK will be wetter winters with heavier rainfall leading to flooding, soil erosion and waterlogged soil, which all affect plant growth. The amount of flooding has increased greatly over the last five years and will continue to get worse. Waterlogged soils can kill plants or at best restrict and stunt growth, resulting in poor flowering and fewer crops. Regular waterlogging considerably restricts the range of plants that can be grown and very few are plants that will produce a crop.

During the summer more droughts are predicted, again leading to poorer growth and lower yields as well as restricting the range of plant species that will grow and thrive. There are likely to be more storms causing damage to plants, especially if they are in full leaf. Damaged plants are more susceptible to be attacked by diseases, making plant care more difficult. Storms also result in damage to greenhouses, polytunnels, sheds and other garden buildings, as well as serious soil erosion if windy, and dry soil also reduces soil fertility. Although not predicted to be frequent, heatwaves cause damage to many plants, which tend to shut down when temperatures reach 30°C as this seriously affects enzyme processes within them.

To slow down and eventually stop climate change, many countries agreed at COP26 to be net zero CO_2 producers by 2050. According to climate scientists this is achievable, although progress has been very slow so far. To achieve this target will require everyone to make changes to their lifestyle and needs leadership from governments, organisations, companies and individuals. As individuals we can make a number of changes, some of which are covered later in this book, but non-gardening ones include flying less, making fewer car journeys, using electric- or hydrogen-powered cars, reducing energy use in homes, increasing renewable energy and generally moving towards a more sustainable lifestyle.

We cannot continue with 'business as usual' and hope to thrive or even survive in the future. We need to adapt now to reduce our use of carbon and the amount of carbon dioxide, nitrous oxide and methane we are producing, which are key factors in the cause of climate change. We need to start living more sustainable lives now and make further changes into the future to take better care of the environment and develop more biodiversity.

If we are to live on this planet long term, we need to learn how to make changes and actually make them; we need to truly address the issue of climate change and not be overawed by or depressed by the situation. Action *will* make a difference. You can start in the garden and house by making small changes to reduce energy use, grow more food, recycle waste, compost green waste and more.

THE EFFECTS OF CLIMATE CHANGE ON THE GARDEN

Drought

The first effect of climate change on the garden is drought. This was driven home in the UK by the summer of 2022 – or for those that remember it, 1976! Although 2022 had some heavy showers, the overall amount of rain was well down on the normal UK average, resulting in long, dry periods, which were worsened by very hot weather in July and August. Many lawns went brown, young plants and bedding plants died (unless watered daily) and others failed to make the growth they usually did, giving smaller plants. Large numbers of vegetables failed to produce a crop, or if they did it was a much smaller crop than expected. It was dry for so long it was not possible to sow replacement crops unless irrigation was available.

Droughts are predicted to become more frequent and last longer. This will have an effect on the choice of plants that can be grown and yields of fruit and

Allium
'Globemaster'.

Fabiana
imbricata.

Hosta 'Big Daddy'.

Wisteria floribunda 'Macrobotrys.

vegetables, which will affect food prices. Drought is not just caused by higher temperatures but also long periods without rain, lower total rainfall and increased winds, which both dry the soil by evaporation and increase plant transpiration as the wind or breeze draws moisture from the leaves.

Higher Temperatures

Higher temperatures are also predicted as a result of climate change. These were also witnessed in 2022 in the UK, with the highest temperature on record achieved in July and several days with very high temperatures.

High temperatures not only dry out the soil but they increase the plant transpiration rate, meaning the plants need more water, which often is not available. Some of the plants growing in the UK have not evolved or adapted to high sunlight and these can be sun scorched, resulting in dead patches on the leaves. In future, we need to choose plants that have adapted to the high levels of sunlight and temperatures – these will be plants from Mediterranean climates or even warmer areas of the world.

More Storms

Climate change has resulted in more storms, and these are of a greater severity than many in the past. Again, 2022 was a good example as the UK suffered storms Malik, Corrie, Dudley and Eunice; two of which were very severe in the south of England, causing a lot of damage to gardens.

If storms become more common, we will need to take action to reduce their effects on gardens. While it is not possible to stop storms and prevent all damage, it is possible to reduce the damage caused, which will be covered later (*see* Chapter 7).

Increasing Rain

More frequent and heavier rain is also expected – the complete opposite of drought! This is likely to occur in the winter and could build up in the soil to the point of causing waterlogging, soil erosion and flooding. Soil can absorb large amounts of water, which slowly percolates down to the water table, but if too much rain falls in a short period of time, it cannot percolate through the soil fast enough and runs off, causing soil erosion and then flooding. Flooding is devastating for homeowners and businesses and for that reason alone we should be doing everything possible to reduce it.

The flooding of gardens and allotments can result in them being contaminated by sewage, which means any vegetables in the area will be inedible. The garden will also need cleaning up before it is usable again. We need to help the soil hold more water, which will reduce flooding and also delay the effects of drought.

Milder Winters

Milder winters are another likely effect of climate change. At first glance, this may seem a plus point.

However, there are some negative consequences for gardeners – the main one being that many fruits grown in the UK require a period of cold to help initiate flower buds and ensure a decent level of fruit. The amount of cold is measured in day degrees and each fruit has a set requirement of day degrees, which is made up of a period of time below a set temperature. If, owing to the mild winter, there are insufficient day degrees, fruit yields will be reduced. In the future, scientists will be able to breed fruit that needs a lower day degree level, but it will mean that some of the well-loved cultivars are no longer suitable, including many heritage varieties.

Another unwanted side effect of milder winters will be more pests overwintering, meaning we will need to be more vigilant and have good control methods ready. It is also possible that new pests and diseases will spread over from Europe or even other parts of the world; in earlier years they would have been killed by cold winters, but in the future this will not be the case.

The last few years have also seen drier springs, which has delayed sowing, making the plants more prone to drought damage in the summer.

Wildfires

One of the results of climate change has been more forest fires and wildfires throughout the world, including in the UK. Vast areas have been burnt, resulting in more carbon – as well as heat and other pollutants – going into the air, and the death of many creatures.

WHAT CAN WE DO?

We are leaving the planet in a mess for our children, grandchildren and great-grandchildren and we need to start to take action *now* to change our lifestyles, otherwise catastrophe will occur in the future. We need to live more sustainable lives and use more sustainable materials, especially those using low amounts of carbon to produce.

One simple action we can take is to grow more vegetation to cool the environment, especially trees and shrubs. More needs to be done to reduce flooding and the damage and misery it causes by making use of permeable paving, swales and other techniques to hold water on or in the soil.

Chapter 4 gives a number of techniques to encourage us to use water wisely, conserving and recycling where we can. In the future we should consider making greater and better use of sewerage, even if it is just to reduce the amount going into the rivers and coastal sea.

As well as adding insulating and installing solar panels to our buildings – whether homes, garages, sheds or outbuildings – consider whether they could support a roof garden, which reduces water loss from the roof and provides an area of biodiversity, as well as absorbing some CO_2. Buildings also provide support and shelter for climbing plants and shrubs, especially tender plants, which will change in the future as the UK climate warms up. South-facing walls could be ideal sites for exotic fruits.

We can make sustainable changes by reducing our energy use when we garden, using hand equipment where possible rather than petrol; either electric or preferably battery-powered machines, especially if they are charged by their own solar panel.

Growing your own fruit and vegetables is something nearly everybody can do, even if it is just a few salad leaves or microgreens on the windowsill. This reduces the carbon footprint, food miles and the importing of vegetables from countries that need to use large valuable amounts of water to grow them. Growing your own is both physically and mentally good for you, giving you fresh food, saving you money and benefitting the climate and planet Earth. If you do not have a garden, have a go at foraging as it is surprising what food can be foraged from the land in the UK, even in cities.

Agriculture accounts for 14 per cent of greenhouse gas emissions and according to a UN survey the average British diet could be responsible for 8.8 kilos of CO_2 equivalent emissions per person every day. To help reduce this, we need to reduce the amount of meat and dairy we eat and drink. Changing to a more plant-based diet, preferable home grown, and reducing meat consumption will improve our health and help the planet. We need to create more resilient food systems to reduce the likelihood of food shortages by growing more in the UK and, if possible, at home. This will make us less susceptible to likely food shortages in the future.

Hopefully reading this book will encourage you to take action, make changes to your own garden and live a more sustainable life.

CHAPTER 1

GARDEN DESIGN

When designing, constructing and maintaining a garden over many years, numerous choices can be made to reduce its carbon footprint. Choose sustainable materials and plants that do not require too much maintenance, especially by machinery using non-renewable energy. Consider what materials, artefacts (if any) and other non-plant additions to the garden you would like to include and ask yourself: are they really necessary and sustainable?

If we are to make any effect in reducing climate change, we need to make our lifestyles more sustainable. Importing stone from India is not sustainable or necessary as there is perfectly good attractive stone available in the UK – using this will reduce the carbon footprint of the garden construction, not to mention the balance of payments on importing and exporting! Try to keep inclusion of outside materials, other than plants, into the garden to a minimum and any hard landscaping should be sustainable and allow the drainage of water (SuDS compliant).

SITE SURVEY AND APPRAISAL

The first stages of garden design are the site survey and appraisal. These are carried out to ascertain what is on

the site and the size, shape and levels of the site. All of these are important when designing a garden that is going to be resilient in the face of a changing climate.

Basic information about the site is collected and stored in a notebook or on a laptop or tablet. The type of information to gather includes:

- **Existing buildings:** houses, garages, sheds, greenhouse outbuildings
- **Existing plants:** trees, shrubs, hedges, herbaceous plants – are they worth retaining?
- **Boundaries:** position, form of boundary (hedge, fence, wall)
- **Soil:** types (sand, silt, clay, chalky), pH, depth, condition (*see* Chapter 2)
- **Existing hard surface areas:** drives, paths, parking areas, patios – can they be retained or reused?
- **Other features:** views from the site, water features, ornaments

Adjacent Land Use and Topography

Look at the surrounding area. Does it slope? If so, which way? If it slopes towards your garden, is it likely that water is going to enter it? Where will any water flow?

Note the surrounding land: how high or low is your ground and the ground surrounding it? If it looks likely that water could flow into your garden (and possibly your house), what can be done to prevent this? At the design stage it is easy to incorporate swales, berms, ditches, drains, ponds, wet areas and rain gardens, rather than adding them later. Consider the use of raised beds if the land is likely to be wet for long periods.

Whether your garden is a new or an existing site, survey it or have it professionally surveyed and designed. A new site is likely to be a blank canvas, possibly apart from retained trees, so it can be designed from scratch. If it is an existing garden or you are redeveloping your garden, try to retain any existing trees if they are healthy, and possibly some shrubs too. This gives the garden a mature feel and retains any carbon within the trees and shrubs.

Clearing the Area

Try not to carry out wholesale demolition without thinking through the consequences; one of which will be a lot of waste, unless the materials can be reused. Waste is both expensive to dispose of and wasteful in resources, so consider retaining buildings that are in good condition. Demolition waste like hardcore can be used as a base for drives, paths, patios and buildings, thus saving money and carbon footprint. Wood can be used as biomass for heating, if it is not suitable for other uses. Any plant waste can be composted or used in a *hügelkultur* (*see* Chapter 6). Your aim should be to clear the site with the lowest possible carbon footprint and zero waste.

Many plants, even semi-mature trees, can be moved if prepared properly. Small trees and medium-sized shrubs are reasonably easy to move and replant onsite or elsewhere. Most small shrubs and herbaceous plants are easy to lift and transplant – this should be done in the autumn or winter.

Any plants removed should be recycled by composting the soft green material; use any woody material for habitats for wildlife or as biomass. Perennial weed roots can be put into a bucket or an old paint tin, half-filled with water, where they will rot and can then be added to the compost heap. Where possible, retain any mature plants that will fit in with the design as they will help to give the garden instant maturity and – in the case of trees – will already be sequestering carbon.

Any topsoil should be retained onsite – it is too valuable a material to have carted away. Even removing subsoil is not sustainable and should be kept onsite for grading out to get the levels required before covering with topsoil. If wildflower areas are wanted, these are better sown on subsoil as it has low fertility and tends to produce better-flowering plants, whereas topsoil can be too fertile and produces lush leaf growth and many coarse weeds but fewer flowers.

Buildings other than sheds, greenhouses and polytunnels are not easy to move, but before demolishing them consider if they can be used or converted to another use. For example, an old barn could make a good garage or storage area. If the buildings have no use or are not required and are demolished, before carting the debris offsite consider if it could be used onsite, which will reduce transport costs and the carbon footprint. Metal can be recycled via scrap merchants and wood has many uses, from biomass through to uses in the garden.

Your aim should be to clear the area with the lowest possible carbon footprint and zero waste; unless the site has been contaminated in the past, nearly everything onsite should be reusable in some form. Try to make this point to any architects, builders and contractors involved – certainly builders are notorious for creating waste from materials that still have value. If you intend to have wildflower or natural areas, can some of the original plants be retained? There is no point in clearing grasses, scrub and trees if you wish to create a natural area – just retain the existing plants with possibly some selective thinning or removal of unwanted species.

DESIGN CONSIDERATIONS

Whether you design the garden yourself or engage a garden designer may depend on your budget, time available and skills. Either way, aim for as sustainable a design as possible using the minimum of hard landscape materials – not too large a formal lawn and an area for growing vegetables and possibly fruit. Choose the right plants for the right places, so they thrive and do not require expensive maintenance.

If building from scratch, is it worth incorporating a permanent irrigation system using low water-use systems and an underground storage tank? These keep water use to a minimum, yet lead to healthy plant growth. They have little or no maintenance, and once installed no costs (other than the water, which, if collected from the roof, is free). Aim to design a garden that requires the minimum use of water by including gravel, xeriscape (*see* later in this chapter) and dry gardens. If the garden is in a wet area, grow plants that are adapted to these conditions. This is more sustainable than constantly having to maintain them and/or installing a drainage scheme.

Features to include in the garden will depend on your personal choice, although some may be dictated by the site, soil or location. If the site is wet or prone to flooding then swales, raised beds, rain gardens, ponds and other similar features will be useful. If the garden is located in the drier eastern side of the UK, lack of water may be a bigger problem and water collection in large tanks, ponds, water butts, irrigation systems in the soil and other similar equipment will be useful.

We will look at some of the features to include in a new or renovated garden below:

Hard Landscaping

In the past, garden designers have used too much hard landscaping materials in their designs. This is not sustainable and should be reduced. In areas of high rainfall, like Wales and the western side of England and Scotland, hard landscaping should be kept to a minimum – this gives a greater area to grow plants, which is what gardening is really about. Ensure any water can either permeate through the hard landscaping or the surrounding areas can absorb it. Otherwise leave gaps in the hard landscaping area for water to penetrate and plant these with low-growing plants like thymes or some alpines. Try to break up larger areas of hard landscaping with planted areas or trees in pits. These will collect water and allow it to drain into the soil.

Leaving aside the question of how much energy is used in the making or quarrying and transporting of hard landscape materials, which all add to the effects of climate change, let us consider the use of hard landscaping in the garden. As mentioned above, the less used the better, as this gives a greater area for water percolation and planting, which gives the garden a more relaxed feel. Many front gardens have been covered in tarmac, concrete or block pavers, which

forces any water out onto the highways, consequently causing flooding once the drainage system is full (they were not designed to take water from the gardens, only the highways). Any hard landscaped areas included in your garden should have sustainable drainage systems (SuDS). This will mean they will cope with rainwater locally (within the garden, if possible), rather than pushing the problem further downstream, causing flooding. Aim to mimic the natural drainage of soils and woodlands so the water infiltrates into the soil. Good examples of SuDS include: permeable paving, swales, rain gardens, wet gardens or bog gardens.

It is possible to have paved parking spaces that allows water to percolate and plants to grow, giving a more attractive area. The area that the car will actually drive over or park on can be paved, but the area between the wheels can be planted with low-growing plants and either side of the parking area can also be planted. An alternative is to use porous paving, grass-crete (either with concrete or plastic grids for support) that will hold the weight of a car or van, or block pavers with narrow gaps between for water to pass through. Porous paving is available, which allows water to pass through, drain into the sub-base and then down into the subsoil; there are types of porous asphalt and concrete that can be supplied and laid by contractors.

Attractive paths can be constructed from bricks set with a 6mm (¼in) gap between each one, allowing water to enter; the same can be done with setts or pavers. Ensure they are laid onto a free-draining but firm base of crushed stone and sand. Over time, moss may grow in the gaps but this can easily be brushed off – some people consider moss to be attractive, giving a feel of maturity while water can still percolate through.

The carbon footprint of the design can be reduced by using natural stone or, even better, recycled stone, rather than concrete or tarmac. Although natural stone may be more sustainable if quarried locally, it is still expensive and you should consider the damage it does to the countryside. Having said that, using a local stone or material is far better than importing stone from India or other Asian countries – this is not sustainable and has a massive carbon footprint, so should be avoided.

Aggregates and gravels are useful for drives, paths and larger areas, and they are permeable and cheaper than many of the other hard landscaping materials. They are easy to lay and require little maintenance other than the occasional weeding and raking to keep them loose. After a number of years, they may need topping up where they have worn thin. There are a range of materials that can be used including pea gravel, shingle, slate chippings, seashells, glass and rubber crumbs. Also there are the self-binding gravels like Bredon gravel, which are laid over a hardcore base. Self-binding gravels are a mixture of aggregate, sand and clay and are laid to a depth of 7.5–10cm (3–4in), levelled and compacted. They form an even, hard-wearing surface for paths, cycle tracks and even car parks. They can sometimes form puddles on low-lying areas, but these will drain in a day or so.

Decking, usually made of wood, has become common in many gardens over the last twenty or thirty years. I have to admit to never being keen on it as I feel there are better uses for wood, especially if imported from halfway around the world. Even the best timber has a limited life span and is often slippery after rain or heavy dew. Underneath the decking also offers the perfect home for the local rat population! Having said that, timber is a sustainable and renewable material and can be reasonably priced, as well as locking up carbon in the wood. Decking can be an attractive feature and may blend into the garden well. It will need treating with preservative at intervals to prevent rotting – avoid using toxic chemicals but choose a natural preservative. Ensure any wood is FSC certified and not from illegal logging.

An alternative to wooden decking is the recycled plastic type of timber made from recycled plastic bottles. This is commonly available in black and dark brown and looks reasonably wood-like. It makes use of recycled plastic and is long-lasting as well as rot proof.

Moving away from the surface or horizontal hard landscaping, vertical hard landscaping includes features such as fences, walls (both boundary and internal), trellises, pergolas, arches and other structures. Again, try to use sustainable and/or recycled materials. Although, at first glance, wooden fences may seem a more sustainable option than walls, they need annual treatment to prevent rotting, often using chemicals, and will eventually rot and need replacing. Brick, stone or block walls may have a high carbon footprint but they will last a lifetime without any maintenance, other than repointing once every twenty years.

If using timber, choose either FSC-approved timber or natural timber from local woodlands or coppices that will last a few years and then be replaced with similar wood – this will be a choice made at the design stage.

Trees

We all need to plant more trees. The British government set a target to plant 30 million trees by 2030, but is well behind target at present. There are charities such as The Woodland Trust, National Trust, Trees for Cities and others who are planting many trees on their land – and if you do not have space for a tree, they will be happy for you to help plant some for them!

Trees are very important as they are the largest plants so will absorb the most carbon dioxide and produce the most oxygen. They are also excellent in reducing air pollution, as the particulates from the air land on the leaves and are either washed off by rain onto the ground or stay on the leaf until it drops onto the ground, thus leaving the air cleaner. Trees can reduce the air temperature by 2–8°C, which during hot periods like the summer of 2022 can make a big difference to people who are struggling. In urban areas, this reduces the heat island effect where the heat builds up during the day and remains high overnight, making the atmosphere unpleasant and sleep difficult.

During rain, especially heavy rain, trees can intercept up to 30 per cent of the water. In the summer, much will be evaporated back into the atmosphere, reducing the risk of flooding. Trees also slow the speed of rain, which slows soil erosion and delays the water reaching the drains, again reducing the risk of flooding. Trees provide shade and reduce the amount of heat entering buildings, keeping homes or buildings pleasant while reducing the need to use energy for air conditioning.

Climbing Plants and Wall Shrubs

Climbers are an underutilised group of plants that can add an extra dimension to the garden and make use of an area that is often wasted or not used – that of walls (both buildings and boundary, also internal walls, if any), fences and screens. They provide a habitat for a wide range of insects and birds and also have a greening effect as they improve the appearance of the vertical dimension, as well as screening unsightly structures. Many climbers provide flowers, colourful leaves, fruits and autumn colour; some are deciduous

Small Trees Suitable for Domestic Gardens

- *Acer davidii*
- *Acer griseum*
- *Acer japonicum*
- *Acer palmatum*
- *Amelanchier lamarckii*
- *Cornus kousa*
- *Cornus* 'Porlock'
- *Crataegus laevigata* 'Pauls Scarlet'
- *Crataegus prunifolia*
- *Cydonia oblonga* 'Vranja'
- *Ilex* × *altaclerensis*
- *Juniperus communis* 'Hibernica'
- *Laburnum* × *watereri* 'Vossii'
- *Magnolia* × *soulangeana*
- *Magnolia stellata*
- *Malus* 'Evereste'
- *Malus* 'Golden Hornet'
- *Malus* 'John Downie'
- *Pinus mugo*
- *Prunus* 'Cheal's Weeping'
- *Prunus* 'Pandora'
- *Prunus* 'Tai Haku'
- *Rhus typhina*
- *Sorbus aucuparia*
- *Sorbus aucuparia* 'Fructo Luteo'
- *Sorbus hupehensis*
- *Sorbus* 'Joseph Rock'
- *Sorbus vilmorinii*
- *Syringa vulgaris* 'Charles Joly'

While on the subject of using the walls of houses and other buildings, south-facing walls and fences are a valuable location for growing plants needing a warm microclimate. Although climate change is resulting in higher temperatures, there will always be plants on the borderline of hardiness in the UK that we wish to grow, and south-facing areas are ideal for this. We can currently grow apricots, peaches and nectarines, but there will be other plants that may grow in parts of the country including possible *Bougainvillea* and similar plants.

As well as climbing plants – most of which are shrubs, with a few annuals available – there are other

Apricot delicot 'Flavorcot' – one of the new breed of apricots that will produce good crops, even in the UK, and will likely improve with climate change.

Nectarines – a great plant for a south-facing wall, making good use of the space. Again, crops are likely to improve with climate change.

and others evergreen; and there is a range of plants available for any aspect, from north to south and east to west.

As well as absorbing CO_2, climbing plants and wall shrubs have an insulating effect on buildings, helping to reduce heat loss from walls on cold, especially windy, days. They also have a cooling effect on hot summer days, which are more likely to occur in the future. This will reduce the need for air conditioning – a large energy user. Any bare walls can be covered by climbers – some of which will cling and are self-supporting; others will need a trellis or wires for support.

Peaches are related to apricots and nectarines and like similar conditions. As the climate warms, peaches will become easier to grow.

Rhodochiton atrosanguineus 'Bell Vine' – an attractive, fast-growing annual, useful for giving quick colour in borders.

Thunbergia alata – another annual climber for quick colour, which will grow up trellises, obelisks or other supports.

shrubs and a few trees that can be grown against walls. These help to reduce the harsh effect of buildings and tie them into the landscape, as well as adding interest and colour. Common annual climbers include *Lathyrus* (sweet pea), *Cobaea scandens*, *Rhodochiton atrosanguineus* and *Thunbergia alata*; the runner and French beans are both decorative and will produce a good crop. Shrubs commonly grown as wall shrubs that work very effectively are *Garrya elliptica*, *Euonymus fortunei*, *Chaenomeles japonica*, *Jasminum*, *Fremontodendron* and *Carpenteria*.

These are all decorative, give an extra dimension and help the house and other buildings to blend into the garden, as well as having a good insulating effect both in summer and winter, which will be important as climate change takes effect. They are also useful to screen boundary walls and fences and to act as windbreaks on windy sites (reducing the effects of windstorms, which are likely to become more frequent). Covering boundaries with planting helps to give greater depth to the garden as it leads the eye further, making the space appear bigger to the eye than it actually is.

Fruit Trees

Starting with the trees, only dwarf trees should be used to avoid damage to the building foundations. Walls are an ideal location for fruit trees. At a time of expensive food and the need to reduce food imports and give

Parthenocissus quinquefolia (Virginia Creeper) – a rampant shrubby climber that will cover large walls or other areas. It has a very good red autumn colour.

Ficus carica (Fig) – large bold leaves give a dramatic effect. It will not only cover the wall but will also produce fruit. Yields are likely to improve as climate change progresses.

Pears – another fruit that can be wall-trained as cordons or espaliers. They make very good use of wall space, look attractive when in flower and produce a good crop.

better self-sufficiency, growing your own fruit is well worth considering.

The range of fruit trees suitable for growing against a wall include apples, pears, cherries, plums, and on south-facing walls: peaches and nectarines. Figs are also very useful and grow well in poor dry soils, which against a wall is often the case. They have large decorative foliage and in the late summer produce edible fruit, which is highly prized.

The amount of fruit that can be harvested from wall-trained fruit trees is surprising. Fruit trees can be purchased ready trained or as young whips to be trained into shape. Espalier, cordon and fan fruit trees can be trained into fancy 'S' shapes, rings, columnar, or whatever takes your fancy! They just need their branches tied to wire and regular summer (and sometimes winter) pruning.

Hedges

Looking at boundaries, many modern gardens have fences to demarcate the boundary. However, with the increase of stormy weather, these will be prone to blowing down or being damaged by severe winds, especially once they start to age and the posts begin to rot. Hedges, on the other hand, tend to stay firm. Rather than acting as a block to the wind, they filter it, so are less likely to be damaged (apart from having a few leaves blown off).

Hedges can be deciduous, evergreen or mixed, and grown to any height you desire, although it requires time for the plants to reach 2m (6½ft) or more (instant hedging can be bought if you are impatient or need an instant effect). They provide nesting sites for birds, a habitat for some mammals and a wide range of insects, as well as being a lot more sustainable than fences or walls and they will last a lot longer if properly maintained. If bought as small plants, they are also a lot cheaper than fencing or walls and will absorb CO_2 as they grow. Some will provide flowers and fruit, and variegated leaved versions are also available. They look far more interesting than walls or fences and add an extra dimension to the garden, as well as greater depth.

Most hedges are reasonably quick growing and will form a screen in three to four years. If instant privacy is required, a temporary windbreak can be erected, which will give protection and privacy until the hedge is established. Hedges are long-lasting – some have lasted for hundreds of years – and give a very sustainable boundary screen. They filter the wind, reducing its speed, and help to protect the garden and plants, even during storms.

A 2m- (6½ft-) high hedge will offer very good protection for a small- to medium-sized garden and, if kept clipped and narrow, does not take up much space. Even a lower hedge up to 1m (3¼ft) high will give some protection to a small area of plants – these would be useful as internal hedges on windy sites.

Hedges can be planted in a single line of plants for a narrow but dense hedge. If a thicker hedge is required to prevent animal access, or on a really windy site, a double staggered row can be planted. This uses more plants so costs more, but it provides a very dense hedge. Most urban hedges are a single species, such as an all yew or beech hedge. They can also be mixed like many rural hedges, especially if a native hedge is wanted, which gives greater diversity and a mix of flowers and fruits.

Maintenance involves just cutting one to four times a year, depending on the species of hedge and the required standard. One cut per year is sufficient for some hedges, like beech and hornbeam, as it will be for rural or natural hedges. Nowadays, hedge cutting is reasonably easy with mechanical cutters, especially battery-operated types. If possible, avoid the hedge getting too tall and wide as this makes cutting difficult. Access equipment may be required unless long-reach hedge cutters are available.

There is a good range of plants available for hedging. Try to purchase bare root plants rather than container-grown plants, which are a lot more expensive; although evergreen species are usually only container grown. Suitable plants include:

- Beech – *Fagus sylvatica*
- Hornbeam – *Carpinus betulus*
- Hazel – *Corylus avellana* gives nuts, if you beat the squirrels
- Privet – *Ligustrum ovalifolium*
- Portuguese laurel – *Prunus lusitanica*
- Laurel – *Prunus laurocerasus*
- Conifers like *Thuja*, *Lawsoniana* and *Leylandii*

For dwarf internal hedges, lavender, rosemary and cotton lavender are very good and drought resistant.

Alder (*Alnus glutinosa*) – used as a windbreak and tall hedge, trimmed once a year using hand- or tractor-mounted machinery.

If a tall hedge is required to screen adjacent houses or an unsightly structure in the distance, an alternative to hedging is pleached trees, which are basically a hedge on stilts. The trees can be purchased ready pleached or as young saplings, two to three years old, and trained. A pleached tree has a trunk of 1.8m (6ft), all the branches are trained horizontally on two sides of the trunk and all growth comes from these horizontal branches. They form a narrow screen the width of a typical hedge and are trimmed annually to maintain their size and shape. Plants that are commonly pleached include hornbeam, lime, beech and even holly.

Dead Hedges

Another option to consider for boundaries and screening is the dead hedge, sometimes referred to as a fedge (more on this later). These are very useful and sustainable. As well as being instant like a fence, they are made using waste prunings and similar material, which can be difficult and expensive to dispose of. They provide a very good habitat for birds and other creatures, as well as some fungi, and can easily be greened up using annual climbers.

Dead hedges are very easy and fairly quick to make; simply put a garden line along where the centre of the hedge needs to be, mark this with sticks or spray can paint then remove the line. Measure 30–60cm (12–24in) either side of the centre (depending on how wide you want your hedge) and mark again with sticks or paint. Now hammer in 1m (3¼ft) stakes or straight branches (or taller for a tall hedge) approximately every 1.5m (5ft) apart along both lines. The space between the two lines is filled with the prunings and branches, which should be pushed down and firmed in place. Dead hedges over 1m (3¼ft) require a stake to be hammered through the prunings into the soil to hold it stable. Once it is finished it looks like a recently laid hedge. It can be left like this or climbers can be planted to grow through and over the dead hedge to give the appearance of a living hedge.

Another advantage of dead hedges is that the carbon in the prunings is locked in the wood and not released by burning. As the wood rots, the carbon gets incorporated into the soil below, locking it up for many years. Dead hedges will last for five or more years but if topped up with fresh prunings will go on forever and is a useful way of using a waste material. There is no clipping or other maintenance required and it provides

Dead hedge – a very useful method of creating a quick barrier or boundary at a low cost, making good use of waste prunings.

an excellent habitat for many creatures so is good for biodiversity.

Fedges

I mentioned fedges in the previous section as a word sometimes used to describe a dead hedge. The same word, confusingly, is also used by others to describe a wire or chain-link fence that is covered in climbing plants. This forms a very narrow hedge, hence the name fedge: a mixture of fence and hedge. They are useful in small gardens as they provide a screen without taking up the space a hedge would. Climbing plants can be annuals like sweet peas, *Cobaea*, *Thunbergia*, runner and French beans; nasturtiums or perennials like ivy, with both plain green or variegated leaves available, clematis, vines, honeysuckle and so on. These will provide flowers and again a habitat for many creatures and are far more sustainable than a post and wire fence.

To make a fedge, erect the post and wire or chain-link fence as usual then plant the required plants along the fence at 1–3m (3¼–10ft) spacings, depending on the plant chosen. Train the plants up the wire to start, then they will climb naturally. Fedges form an attractive boundary fence that requires little maintenance (no fence painting!) and adds interest to the garden, especially for the small gardens typical of most modern houses.

One other type of hedge or screen that is sometimes called a fedge is a living willow hedge made using willow rods. This is not quite instant but is quick growing – it does not take long to form a dense screen that can be pruned annually or as required. Willow is also a good plant for wet and clay soils.

This hedge is made using willow cuttings from 90cm (35in) to 2m (6½ft) in length, which can be purchased or cut from existing plants. They are just pushed into the ground to 20–30cm (8–12in) for the smaller cuttings or 60cm (24in) for the very large cuttings. If planted during the winter, they will root in the spring and be growing by early summer. The cuttings can range from 1cm (½in) diameter for the smaller, younger ones to 5–7cm (2–2¾in) for the larger, older cuttings. Put down a line to mark the position of the hedge and push in some of the thicker cuttings

2m (6½ft) apart, then divide the remaining cuttings in half and put half in at a 45° angle sloping one way and the remaining half at a 45° angle in the opposite direction. If thin material is used, it can be woven together to give it strength; if using thicker material they should be self-supporting but can be tied together if required. The same technique can be used to retain watercourse banks or can be made into arches or similar structures.

Planting

Up until recently the planting season for bare root trees, shrubs and roses was from November (it used to be October!) to late March or early April. However, with the recent dry springs, which seem to be becoming more frequent, an autumn planting is to be recommended. Autumn planting also has the advantage that the plants can get partly established over winter, before the really dry and hot weather of the summer arrives. If the winters continue to stay milder this will help the plants to become established as the roots can grow for longer.

To ensure plants are to grow and thrive it is more important than ever that the ground is thoroughly prepared before planting by deep digging and incorporating as much organic matter as possible, followed by breaking up any lumps. If the ground is compacted or panned in any way these should be broken using a fork or even a Kango-type machine to ensure free drainage and good aeration.

Soak any bare root and container-grown plants before planting to make sure they are not dry. Ensure the roots are not damaged during planting and prune off any that are damaged; the plant needs all the roots it has to extract water from the soil. If a container-grown plant is pot-bound, the trend has been to make massive cuts into the root ball to encourage new roots – this is a bit drastic and may do more harm than good. It is far better to try to tease out as much root as possible, cutting any that are damaged to give a clean cut. If any number of roots are removed, it would be wise to prune the top growth back to match and help balance the root shoot ratio of the plant. The more roots it has, the better the chance of the plant thriving.

Mycorrhizal Fungi

A recent trend (recent in the history of gardening!) has been to use mycorrhizal fungi when planting, I would greatly endorse this, having used it on a couple of occasions on sites with poor soil texture and structure. The plant roots were dipped into a paste made of the mycorrhizal powder and then planted. There was 100 per cent establishment, and all 400 plants grew very well and are still doing so. Mycorrhiza help the roots absorb more water as well as nutrients and give the plant some protection from stress and disease attack.

Ensure the plant is planted at the correct depth, firmed in and watered if the soil is dry. Apply a mulch to conserve any water and reduce weed growth, ensuring this mulch does not touch the plant's bark. During the first two to three years, continue to water during dry periods and apply at least 10 litres (2 gallons) to small trees and 20–40 litres (4½–8¾ gallons) to larger trees; shrubs require at least 5 litres (1 gallon). It is better to apply two heavy waterings a week rather than many lighter waterings – most of which may evaporate and could just encourage surface rooting, which is unwanted.

Shelter

As stated in the introduction, increased wind damage is a likely consequence of climate change so increasing the amount of shelter in the garden will be advantageous to help reduce wind damage. In small, modern urban gardens there may not be much you can do, especially if the garden is surrounded by walls or fences. Any tree or shrub planting should help to reduce turbulence from these, and adding a trellis with plants trained on to the top will reduce the wind speed slightly.

If the front garden is open-plan and you are allowed to plant, add some plants to reduce the wind speed, which will not only protect more delicate plants but will also reduce the heat loss from the house. Reducing wind speed not only reduces damage to plants and property but also reduces transpiration loss from plants, which is important during dry periods. The use of trees, hedges, screens and windbreaks all helps to reduce wind speed.

Xeriscaping

This type of landscape developed in the drier areas of North America but is something we need to consider for the UK now that the climate is becoming drier. Xeriscaping is based partly on desert landscapes and uses plants that have a minimum requirement for water as well as a low-maintenance requirement. Xeriscapes are not to everyone's taste, as many people think they are just cacti and sand or gravel with a few rocks, but they are very sustainable and fit in well with hot summers, providing an interesting landscape. They are low maintenance – up to half the maintenance of normal herbaceous or shrub borders – and give a reasonable biodiversity for creatures that like dry habitats. In the UK it is unlikely they will require any watering as the range of plants used have adapted to growing in very hot and dry conditions. If the existing soil is sandy or gravelly, no additions to it are needed; if clay soil, which is not ideal, some organic matter can be added to help improve the drainage. If hardcore or crushed stone is available, this can also be added.

Cultivate the area prior to planting. This will be your only chance as once the garden is planted and mulched, cultivation will not be possible. Grade out to natural slopes and levels and lay a permeable landscape fabric to reduce weed growth and prevent the stone mixing with the underlying soil as it becomes messy over time. Plant up the area by cutting a cross in the fabric and digging out a hole, then place the plant in the hole, return the soil and firm well, then water. Finally, replace the fabric and cover with mulch – this can be gravel, stone chippings, coarse sand or a similar material that is in keeping with a desert landscape. Mulch to a depth of 5–7cm (2–2¾in); some rocks can be included to create effect but not too many as they absorb heat on hot days, which can make the area even hotter!

The main choice of plants are cacti and succulents, but you are not limited to these and other plants that are suitable can be used, such as grey-leaved plants or others adapted to dry conditions. Typical plants are listed in Chapter 7 and should all be hardy in the UK, especially now climate change is having more effect.

Cacti and succulents used in a bedding display at Kew Gardens – although not a xeriscape garden, it shows how one would look. Some cacti and succulents are now hardy in many parts of the UK.

Beschorneria yuccoides – a hardy succulent that could be used in a xeriscape or gravel garden.

Succulents

Cacti and succulents grow in many arid areas in the world and are native from North America down to Chile and Argentina, as well as from North Africa to South Africa, which has a different range of species. They have evolved to grow in hot, dry climates with low levels of rain, and some areas can be quite cold at night. Species that grow in mountainous or cold areas are likely to be reasonably hardy in the UK and are well worth a try.

Succulents survive by storing water in their leaves or stems, which usually have a waxy covering. In the UK they are happy in full sun and can tolerate temperatures down to 5°C, as long as it is dry and they do not thaw too quickly – this is when cell damage is caused. They dislike wet winters, which are more likely to kill them than the cold (when they can be easily protected by a fleece covering).

The ideal area would be a sunny south-facing slope with a free-draining soil and some shelter from the worst of the winter weather, but this varies depending on which part of the country the garden is located in.

In the southern half of the UK, with the effects of climate change it is likely that succulents will survive in most locations, with the exceptions of really wet areas and frost pockets. If the soil is claylike, succulents grow well in containers, especially clay or terracotta pots, which tend to be drier than plastic pots. If grown in containers, a soil-based growing media like John Innes potting compost is better than peat or peat-free media. Whichever compost is used, add some grit, coarse sand or gravel to improve the drainage and add weight to the container for stability.

Water as required during the summer, just letting the compost dry out before watering, but keep dry over winter – they should not need watering from October to March. Feed with liquid feed between once a fortnight and once a month, with half-strength solution during the summer.

If planting out, do not plant too deep and mulch with gravel or chippings. Prepare the soil by adding stone, gravel or coarse sand, if required. For a clay soil, add some organic matter to open up the structure. For a list of suitable plants, *see* Chapter 7.

CHAPTER 2

SOILS

Over the years, soils have been farmed ever more intensively on both arable and mixed farms and many horticultural production areas, as well as in gardens. This has made them more vulnerable to the threats of climate change; in particular, soil erosion, waterlogging and drought. This has been made worse by the widespread use of artificial fertilisers and underuse of organic matter, which has resulted in soils with a poor structure, low productivity and very low levels of organic matter.

This trend started in the 1960s when artificial fertilisers first became widely used and many growers could get higher crop yields using just fertilisers without organic matter. Yields increased and the application of manures and suchlike was considered unnecessary and costly. What was not considered was that many soils had a reasonable level of organic matter in them – from 3 to 5 per cent – and this sustained the early yields. As this level dropped, growers had to increase the application rates of the artificial fertilisers, which are now very costly in both the price and the environmental effect they are having on the climate.

Following research by many soil scientists, we are now returning to some of the old-fashioned practices of organic growing and using more organic matter on the soil. This will not only improve the soil fertility and crop yields but will also increase the amount of carbon stored in the soil. A good well-developed soil is a major store of carbon and among the top five natural carbon stores on earth, along with the oceans and forests. We should be looking to sequester carbon into the soil by adding organic matter and biochar and also reducing cultivations and considering no-dig. Many arable farmers have reduced their cultivations by using no-till methods and not ploughing – this saves fuel as well as retaining carbon in the soil.

Strawy manure – a good source of organic matter, especially for clay soils. As the straw decomposes it leaves narrow gaps in the soil for aeration and drainage.

Progrow – composted municipal garden waste sold by some local authorities. It has been shredded and screened and is a good source of organic matter and for mulching.

SOIL STRUCTURE AND TEXTURE

Better soil management leads to a healthier soil containing a higher number of microbes and greater biodiversity, as well as producing higher yields. It is also easier to manage than poorly structured soils. Soil *structure* is how the soil forms crumbs, peds and aggregates, while soil *texture* is what the soil is made up of (the sand, silt and clay) and the percentage of each. Soil texture is very difficult to change unless vast amounts of material are used at a high cost. It takes a massive amount of sand to improve a clay soil, with a high cost in transport and labour to deliver and spread it.

Soil structure can be improved and although there can be a cost, it is not massive (it need cost very little if good composting is carried out); we will look more at improving soil structure later in this chapter. Soil structure is important as it affects water flow through the soil, and also air flow/distribution, providing space for roots to grow and for soil fauna and other microbes. It also affects how hard or easy soil cultivations are, as well as soil erosion, leaching of nutrients and drainage.

Good soil structure has an open, friable, crumbly structure with space for root growth. It is free draining but will hold some water and nutrients for plant growth. Soil structure can be affected by the weather, such as wetting, drying, freezing and thawing, and it is

these that help to create the tilth required for sowing and planting. The effect of the frosts, wind and rain form the crumbs of the tilth; the milder winters of recent years along with heavy rain has resulted in lower-quality tilth for sowing and wetter soils that delay sowing and planting as they are colder. Heavy or torrential rain can also result in the leaching out of nutrients and soil erosion, which reduce the fertility of the soil.

Damage to the soil structure is also caused by cultivation when the soil is too wet and by excessive cultivation, for example going over the ground too many times with a rotary cultivator, which smashes the structure. Soil structure is important as plant roots have difficulty growing through poorly structured soils, which can be compacted, and this results in poor-quality plants less able to survive in the dry conditions resulting from climate change. Soil should only be cultivated when it does not stick to your boots or is not too dry and dusty.

Drought cracks – showing the effect of drought on clay soils.

Soil Degradation

Soil degradation is both a cause and a result of climate change. Degraded soils rarely grow good plants and certainly do not produce good crops. Once damaged, it is a slow and expensive process to return degraded soils to their former fertility. Soils can be degraded by heavy rainfall, soil erosion, flooding, waterlogging, severe drought, chemical damage and poor cultivation. Waterlogged soils can produce methane – a powerful greenhouse gas worse than carbon dioxide – which can cause the death of plants and some of the soil fauna.

High temperatures result in high evaporation from the soil, which dries the soil more quickly and increases the loss of organic matter and therefore less carbon sequestration, worsening climate change. Wind also dries the soil and can cause soil erosion, as in the dust bowls of the 1930s in the USA and to some extent in East Anglia, where some of the fenland peats are prone to dust blows.

SOILS AND THE DESIGN STAGE

Soil is a very important part of garden design, unless plants are to be grown hydroponically! When designing a garden or moving into a house with an existing garden, it pays to carry out some simple checks and tests to learn about the garden's soil.

Assessing Soil pH

A pH test kit can be purchased from garden centres or on the internet. This simple test will tell you the soil pH, which affects the range of plants that can be grown in that soil. A low or acidic pH is suitable for ericaceous plants like rhododendrons, camellias, heathers and blueberries, as well as magnolias. An alkaline soil suits clematis, scabious, brassicas, dianthus, geranium and lavenders, among others.

It is better to grow plants that have adapted to a particular pH rather than try to change it or grow plants in unsuitable conditions and have to permanently feed and mollycoddle them. Small changes in the soil pH can be made by adding organic matter over time, or by using sulphur to acidify the pH or lime to raise the pH.

A soil sample can be sent to a laboratory to test the pH and the availability of nutrients like phosphorous, potash and magnesium (others can be requested, if required). Nitrogen can be requested but is not usually given as it can change rapidly, especially over winter and in the spring. It is readily leached out of the soil by rain, which during the winter is increasing, owing to climate change, especially heavy rainfall.

Assessing Soil Texture

Another factor to check is soil texture – whether it is a sand, silt, clay or loam. This is very important as it

New raised beds – becoming more widely used now as part of the no-dig movement and useful on wet soils.

affects the drainage, water and nutrient-holding capability of the soil. As climate change progresses and wetter winters occur, this can lead to waterlogging or, even worse, flooding and heavy nutrient loss from the soil. If the soil is a heavy clay texture it is easier to install drainage, a soakaway or raised beds when the garden is being built or major changes are being made than later.

Sandy soils are very free draining, which results in the loss of nutrients and water. Therefore feeding may be required and large amounts of organic matter should be added to help retain water and nutrients.

While checking the soil texture, look at its structure – how the soil is made up. Is it compacted and very firm or open and free draining? Is the soil made up of a crumbly tilth or many very fine particles? Will it turn to mud when wet or form a cap and reduce water infiltration?

If the soil has a poor structure it will result in poor plant growth, so this needs sorting out before the garden is planted. To check the structure, dig some holes in different parts of the garden approximately 30 × 30cm (12 × 12in) and at least 60cm (24in) deep.

Note how hard the digging is as this is a sign of compaction or pan in the soil. Is there a crust on the surface? If so, this is cap, which will form after heavy rain and drying winds. Are there any signs of rusty flecks in the soil? This is sign of waterlogging. While digging, has the soil smeared or stuck to the spade? This indicates it is heavy clay soil.

Are there any roots lower down in the hole? If not, the soil may be poorly aerated, resulting in poor plant growth. How deep is the topsoil? What type of subsoil is it, how compacted is it and are there any signs of poor drainage?

Leave the hole open for a few days. Does it fill with water – a sign of a high water table or water flowing into it from the surrounding ground? Are there any roots present in the subsoil? Break up some of the soil lumps by hand: are they solid, hard or crumbly? If they are damp, do they smear?

The above information will give a guide to the type and condition of the soil and any treatments that need to be carried out at the construction stage or ongoing during maintenance to maintain and improve it.

NO-DIGGING

No-digging has been known and used for many years – books were written back in the 1940s explaining the technique and its virtues. In recent years, there has been a lot of debate on the advantages and disadvantages of digging verses no-dig growing, especially for vegetables. No-dig growers are becoming more common and many people new to gardening tend to be no-diggers; whether this trend will continue will depend on the yields and crops these gardeners are getting in a few years' time. If the crop quality has been maintained, no-digging will likely increase; but if it has declined, possibly owing to soil compaction and poorer soil structure, no-dig will become less common.

Digging Vs No-Dig

Digging is carried out to:

- Bury crop remains
- Control annual weeds by burying them
- Add organic matter to the soil
- Break any soil pans, surface capping or compaction
- Leave a clean (weed-free) level surface for sowing and planting
- Aerate the soil
- Expose soil pests to predators
- Clear weedy ground quickly
- Be a satisfying and therapeutic technique

Advantages of **no-dig**:

- Digging is not required, saving time and effort
- The organic matter is spread on the surface as a mulch and soil fauna incorporates it
- Earthworms and similar creatures create channels for aeration and drainage
- The soil environment is more stable and soil fungi and microbes build up to a higher level than in dig
- As the soils are not dug and are mulched, there is less chance of erosion
- Fewer weeds grow as the seeds are not brought to the surface by digging
- A stable soil structure is built as it is not damaged by digging
- There is less moisture loss
- It reduces the chance of back problems

Bed covered in compost – either for no-dig purposes or as a mulch.

There are advantages to no-digging if the effects of climate change continue. There is likely to be less soil erosion on no-dig areas, partly as they have a covering of mulch, and also the soil is firmer as it has not been loosened by cultivations.

No-digging makes use of the many micro and macro-organisms in the soil. These replace the digging and appear to benefit the plants, often in a symbiotic relationship. The mulch is added directly to the soil surface, mainly in the autumn, to a depth of 3–15cm (1¼–6in) and will be incorporated into the soil by worms, insects and other creatures and microbes.

The one big disadvantage of no-dig is having a sufficient supply of organic matter for mulching as large amounts are required, even for small gardens. Larger vegetable gardens and allotments can need 2 tonnes or more to be able to mulch the whole area.

Aeration of soil is important as plant roots require oxygen for respiration to grow. This oxygen is in the air space in the soil called the air-filled porosity, which is reduced by walking or using machinery on soil. A good air-filled porosity allows for the drainage of water, movement of air and root growth. It allows water to penetrate the soil more quickly, reducing the amount of runoff, which causes soil erosion and flooding.

There is some evidence that digging or other deep cultivations affect some of the soil microbes and other soil fauna that assist in helping to form the soil structure. Digging disrupts the soil mass including the fungal hyphae, which need to recover and regrow for the next crop or planting. Soils with a good organic content usually have a high microbial activity.

THE IMPORTANCE OF SOIL ORGANIC MATTER

This is a very important topic and it will become more relevant in the future, particularly if soils deteriorate owing to climate change and the need to increase the crop yields for a higher population. We have been aware of the importance of soil organic matter (SOM) for many years, but it has been researched more in recent years and scientists have now realised how important it is in the soil. Soil organic matter is a term used to describe living or once-living material either added to the soil or already in the soil. All organic

The Advantages of SOM

SOM is important for the following reasons:

- It gives the soil structural stability.
- It provides food for earthworms and other soil fauna.
- It provides food for soil microbes and fungi.
- It retains water in sandy soil.
- It helps with drainage in clay soils.
- It provides and holds nutrients.
- Soils with a good organic matter level usually have a high microbial activity.
- It adds and stores carbon in the soil.
- It improves the general health of the soil.

Table 1.1 The Nutrient Content of Some Organic Matter

Material	Nutrient value	Comment
Cattle manure	Nitrogen (N): 0.6 per cent Phosphorus (P): 0.3 per cent Potassium (K): 0.6 per cent	Bullock is best!
Horse manure	N: 0.7 per cent P: 0.3 per cent K: 0.6 per cent	Often freely available in some areas.
Sheep manure	N: 0.7 per cent P: 0.3 per cent K: 0.9 per cent	
Chicken manure	N: 0.7 per cent P: 0.6 per cent K: 0.2 per cent	Mix with other materials.
Pig manure	N: 0.7 per cent P: 0.7 per cent K: 0.5 per cent	Rather wet and smelly!
Homemade compost	N: 2 per cent P: 0.5–1 per cent K: 2 per cent	Will vary depending on what is added to the heap.
Spent hops	N: 0.6 per cent P: 0.2 per cent K: trace	Try some of the new small breweries.
Spent mushroom compost	N: 0.8 per cent P: 0.15 per cent K: 0.54 per cent	
Leaf mould	Very low	The tree absorbs the nutrients before the leaf drops.
Seaweed	N: 0.5 per cent P: 0.1 per cent K: 0.2 per cent	Contains other substances.
Kelp or similar	N: 2–5 per cent P: 0.5 per cent K: 2–5 per cent	
Shoddy	N: 2–10 per cent P: trace K: trace	
Wood ash	N: 0.5–1 per cent P: 2–5 per cent K: 5–15 per cent	Also contains some calcium.
Soot	N: 2–7 per cent P: trace K: trace	
Human hair	N: 12–16 per cent	Ask your barber!
Nettles	N: 3 per cent P: 2 per cent K: 3 per cent	
Comfrey	N: 2 per cent P: 3 per cent K: 5 per cent	Bocking 14 is reputed to be the best.
Eggshells	N: 1 per cent	Also contains some calcium.
Feathers	N: 15 per cent	This is higher than dried blood and hoof and horn.

matter contains carbon – in fact, more than half of it can be carbon; it also includes nitrogen, phosphorous, potassium, sulphur, magnesium and calcium (all of the major nutrients), as well as some micronutrients like copper and zinc.

There is a wide range of organic materials that can be applied to the soil, and these include the following (although there are others available). Use whatever is available at a reasonable price or, better still, free! Table 1.1 shows some of the organic materials available and the typical range of nutrient content that can help to replace expensive fertilisers. The nutrient content varies greatly depending on the source and content of the material, and even on what any animals

have been fed on if it contains animal manure. The figures are from various sources and give a rough guide.

The general rule is to add more organic materials to the soil to increase the organic matter within it. Clay soils need more organic matter than sandy soils to make a similar difference. The organic matter can either be dug or cultivated into the soil, where it decomposes and is used by the many soil fauna, or it can be spread onto the surface and left for the earthworms and other soil creatures to pull into the soil and start the breakdown process. Regular applications of organic matter will act as a mulch as well as being incorporated into the soil to improve the structure.

IMPROVING SOIL STRUCTURE

Surprisingly, whatever the type of soil, the same material will improve its structure and water-holding capacity. That material is organic matter. Whether it is a sandy soil that needs to hold more water for plant growth or a clay soil that needs opening up to allow for better drainage and air porosity, organic matter will make a difference. It will also improve a silt soil by both holding more water and opening it up a little, and it does the same on chalky soils.

Soil organic matter is going to become more important in the future as it will help improve and maintain soil structure, which will make the soil more resilient and less likely to erode in wet conditions. In sandy soils, organic matter will hold water and some nutrients, therefore delaying the onset of drought. In clay soils, organic matter opens up the soil and allows the water to pass through, but also retains some for the plants' use. Whatever type of soil you have, organic

Well-structured soil – an area dug over in the winter and left exposed to the weather to produce a tilth ready for sowing or planting.

matter will improve it, so it is important to add as much as possible at regular intervals, either yearly or bi-yearly. It is unlikely you will add too much.

On clay soils a fresher or coarser organic matter can be used, such as straw, partly decomposed compost, chipped wood and similar. As these decompose, they supply humus to the soil, as well as some nutrition, but leave gaps for water and air to fill, which is good for root growth. Digging in coarse green manures and plant remains are very good for improving heavy soils, particularly if they have thick stems that are slow to decompose. The aim with clay soils is to open them up to allow water and air to pass through but still retain nutrients. Improving clay soils is not a quick fix but a gradual process that leads to a good fertile soil and is well worth the effort. Never work or walk on clay soils if they are wet as it damages the soil structure, which takes a while to improve back to its previous level.

On sandy soils, a more fully decomposed material is better, such as compost, manure, spent hops or spent mushroom compost. These can hold their own weight in water as well as some nutrients, which are released as the material decomposes into humus. The water is freely available to plant roots and each time it rains or the soil is irrigated, the organic matter will reabsorb water, making it available to plants. On sandy soils add as much organic matter as possible over a number of years as it will break down reasonably quickly; it is very unlikely you will add too much, and every bit helps.

The organic matter can be added to the soil by digging (single or double) or mulching, which is used by no-dig growers. The digging can be carried out in the autumn or winter period on all soils, or in the spring only on sandy soils. Mulching is best applied in the spring when the soil is moist after the winter rain but is also warming up with the spring sunshine. On vegetable-growing areas, an autumn application is best so that it is incorporated over winter, ready for sowing or planting in the spring.

Mulching

This is the process of covering the soil with a material that prevents soil water evaporation and therefore reduces the effects of drought. Depending on which material is used, some will also insulate the topsoil to some extent, again reducing the effect of high temperatures as suffered in the summer of 2022. Mulching materials can be split into two main types: organic and inorganic, and they both have their advantages and disadvantages.

Inorganic Mulches

Inorganic mulches are often made from woven plastic materials and include products like MyPex, Plantex and Weed Out. These thin black sheets (like sheets of black polythene) are laid on the soil surface then pegged in place using plastic pins or metal U-shaped pins/staples. They are usually laid prior to planting, pinned down and then the plants are placed into position. Once happy with the position, a cross (X) is cut into the material, a hole dug and a plant placed into it. The soil is pushed back and firmed and then the mulch is replaced and, if required, pinned down. Water the plants if it is dry to get them established. As the black

Pea gravel mulch – a long-lasting non-organic mulch that has an attractive appearance. The obelisk supports for climbers also give height to the border.

MyPex used as a weed control – pinned into the soil, it will prevent weed growth and reduce moisture loss from the soil. In ornamental situations, cover with bark, pea gravel, slate or glass beads to improve the appearance.

mulch does not look very attractive, they are often covered with another material such as gravel, bark, glass beads or slate.

If a bed or border is already planted, it is still possible to lay a sheet mulch. This is best done in the spring when the soil is moist, before the plants start to grow. Lay the mulch along the border and push it around the plants as well as you can. Where the sheet passes a plant, cut the mulch so that it can be fitted around the plant and then pin it into place. It is fiddly but possible, and reduces weed growth as well as water requirement.

Inorganic mulches last for many years and can be walked over without causing any damage. They are available in sheets or rolls (if purchased in rolls they are very competitively priced). The width and length of the rolls vary from 1m (3¼ft) to 2.5m (8¼ft) wide and 10m (11yd) to 100m (109yd) long.

Inorganic mulches are not used by organic growers, but if they wanted to mulch using sheets they could use cardboard or paper for short-term mulches or wool for longer term.

Organic Mulches

Organic mulches use materials that have been partly decomposed and are spread over the soil to a depth of 5–10cm (2–4in), and deeper in some instances. They are best if spread in the spring when the soil is at field capacity (this is when the soil is holding the maximum amount of water it can after drainage). Do not lay if the soil is frozen, frosted or waterlogged. It is best if any weeds are removed before spreading.

There are a range of materials that can be used – some having a better appearance than others. The best is bark, which looks attractive, is sustainable and – if pine bark is used – has a nice smell. It comes in several grades from fine to chunky. Choose a chunky or larger sized grade, which will last longer as it takes longer to decompose. Although expensive, chunky bark will last a number of years and can easily be topped up when required.

The next best material for mulching perennial plantings, like shrubs and mixed and herbaceous borders, is woodchip. This is not as attractive as bark but is a lot cheaper and lasts a similar timespan. Again, use at a minimum depth of 5cm (2in), preferably up to 10cm (4in), and spread in the spring. Like the bark, it should

Strulch mulch – mineralised straw that gives a neat and attractive mulch if applied to 5cm (2in) or thicker.

Woodchip mulch – one of the cheaper mulches, the chipped waste prunings used as a mulch. It is better if it is composted before use to avoid nitrogen deficiency problems.

be composted before using as a mulch, otherwise it will use nitrogen in the soil for decomposing. Although this is released back into the soil after decomposition, it can stunt or slow the growth of your plants. The size of the woodchip can vary, depending on the type and settings on the chipper – a coarser grade is better than a fine grade.

A recycled material that makes a good mulch is cardboard from boxes. These just need to be opened out, laid on the soil and either pinned down or covered with mulch to hold them down. While cardboard can be used on its own, it works better if covered with a bulky material like compost, manure or similar; as the cardboard rots, the other material takes over as the mulch and will need topping up every couple of years. Cardboard is useful in suppressing weeds – even perennial types – as it blocks the light and helps to rot them. Newspaper can also be used but needs to be ten to twenty pages thick to work reasonably well.

Any material that will decompose can also be used if it can be laid over the soil. Hessian-backed carpets like Wilton and Axminster make good mulches. The whole carpet will decompose in time as the top part is wool, which, being a natural material, will decompose. Carpets are fairly long term as they last four to five years, depending on their starting quality.

Bulky materials used for mulching include home-made compost, composted green waste from local authorities, spent hops, spent mushroom compost, well-rotted manure from any farm animal, leaf mould and straw (including Strulch). These can all be applied at 5–10cm (2–4in) deep; the deeper the better as the longer it lasts and the more effective it is as a mulch. The minimum depth of 5cm (2in) will last approximately a year before it decomposes and disappears, whereas 10cm (4in) will last two to three years. It is usually a case of the budget available, as 10cm (4in) will cost twice as much as 5cm (2in). Do not pile the mulch around plant stems – it can cause them to rot as the bark is constantly kept wet.

Ramial Chipped Wood

Ramial chipped wood is woodchip made from the twigs and small branches from hedges, shrubs and trees. It can be used for mulching or soil enrichment; if used as a mulch it is spread over the soil surface to a depth of 5–7.5cm (2–3in). It can be added to the soil like green manure or compost and incorporated into the soil by digging or using machinery on a large scale.

Any young growth up to 7.5cm (3in) diameter can be used for ramial woodchip. It is chipped into small chips (usually smaller than the woodchip supplied by tree surgeons) and in the summer will contain leaves, which help it to decompose. As it is young, thin growth, the wood contains a lot of cambium tissue compared to woody lignified tissue, which normal woodchips contain. Owing to this, the chips are higher in nutrients and decompose more quickly to improve the soil. It is estimated that more than 75 per cent of the nutrients in plants are stored in the twigs.

Apply approximately 2.5cm (1in) of ramial woodchip to the soil and then incorporate it or dig in with green manure, which will help to increase the nitrogen level in the carbon-nitrogen ratio. Fungi tend to break down the woodchip, and bacteria the green manure. Even if ramial woodchip is applied on its own and at higher quantities, it does not appear to cause nitrogen deficiency or nitrogen loss.

It is best to apply ramial woodchip in the autumn so that by the spring, when planting and sowing are likely, any nitrogen lock-up will have disappeared. Ramial woodchip is slower to decompose than green manure, compost or other organic materials, but this can be an advantage as it lasts longer in the soil compared to grass cuttings and similar quick decomposing materials, and this helps to improve the long-term fertility of the soil.

The carbon-nitrogen ratio of ramial woodchip is approximately 30:1 in the thinner twiggy growth, up to 170:1 for the thicker (7cm/2½in) materials. For normal woodchip from large branches and tree trunks, this can be 400:1 up to 750:1, which is why these lock up nitrogen and ramial woodchip does not. Soil fungi break down the wood, releasing any nutrient contained in it – these fungi include some of the mycorrhizae species. Incorporate the woodchip in the top 10–15cm (4–6in) of the soil and try to mix it into the soil so it is spread throughout.

Summer-produced ramial woodchip, which includes a lot of leaves, will heat up when composting, speeding up the decomposition greatly. Once it has cooled it can be applied to the soil. If fresh ramial woodchip is applied in the spring it can cause short-term nitrogen deficiency for a couple of months. This can be avoided by applying a small amount of nitrogen fertiliser or by composting first.

Adding ramial woodchip can make major improvements to a poorer soil in a few years and regular additions maintain that improvement. On very poor soils like subsoil, apply ramial woodchip at 3–4cm (1¼–1¾in) deep and incorporate into the top 5cm (2in) of soil. Do this for three years and then apply 1–2cm (½–¾in) each year after.

Ramial woodchip can be used as a mulch at most times of the year as long as the soil is moist and not frozen. It will reduce weed growth, allow air and water into the soil, retain moisture and store water when it has decomposed. It will also improve soil fertility, increase soil fauna and flora, add carbon to the soil and give a good surface cover.

Ramial woodchip is well worth applying to the soil as it can help to overcome some of the problems associated with climate change like reducing soil erosion, adding and locking carbon in the soil, and improving soil fertility, even of very poor soils. It can be obtained from tree surgeons or you can produce your own using a small electric or petrol chipper to make good use of your pruning waste.

WATERLOGGED SOILS

A waterlogged soil is when all the gaps (pores) between the soil particles are filled with water, rather than a mix of air and water, giving the plant roots access to both oxygen and water. In waterlogged soil, it is not the water that kills the plant but the lack of oxygen for respiration causing the root to shut down and die, after which it starts to rot. The death of the small root hairs is fairly quick and once this happens the plant struggles to take up water, even when the soil drains. Interestingly an early symptom of waterlogging is wilting leaves, as if the plant is suffering from drought.

Even if a plant survives waterlogging, it will be stressed. If this is followed by drought, these plants are often the first to show signs of stress and wilting as they have a smaller root system and cannot absorb sufficient water.

If your soil is prone to waterlogging or has poor drainage it would be wise to improve this by installing drainage or a soakaway, adding a ditch system (think like the Dutch!), using raised beds or, if available, adding sand, grit or stones, although large quantities are required to make much difference. As climate change progresses and we have more wet periods, waterlogging could become worse, so taking some type of action will be worthwhile.

Flooding is becoming more common and extensive, causing millions of pounds worth of damage to property and infrastructure. The main problems with flooding are soil erosion, the loss of good topsoil removed by flood waters, waterlogged soil resulting in plants dying due to lack of oxygen, and contamination of soil by sewerage or industrial pollution. It is likely the government will need to spend billions to reduce future flood events. We can all help to reduce flooding and save people much misery just by making some changes in the garden.

Preventing Flooding

Firstly, reduce the amount of paving or tarmac in the garden. These surfaces are impervious to water, which can only run off into the garden (if lucky), or down the road or drains, adding to flood water further downstream. Try to design or modify the garden to have the maximum permeable area possible, as this will absorb most water up to the point of saturation. Permeable surfaces include grass; gravel; some block paving, grasscrete or similar surfaces; soil; and lawn or grass areas. If the water can be guided to certain parts of the garden where it can be stored temporarily this can help, but avoid it flowing out and flooding your garden, property or neighbour's property.

Try to spread the water over the maximum area possible so it can soak into the soil or other permeable areas. Design your garden so that it has 65–80 per cent permeable surfaced areas – more if possible – and very little water will run off your property. Keeping the soil covered with plants helps to slow down the water movement. Even better is to have layers of plants that the water has to pass through before reaching the soil or ground. The top layer would be trees or large shrubs, followed by small to medium shrubs, then herbaceous plants including groundcover types. These layers both reduce the amount of water reaching the soil and slow it down considerably. Aim to include some evergreens as they provide protection in the winter. Some of the water will evaporate off the plants and never reach the soil; while some will slowly drip down and may take hours to get to the soil, by which time some of the early rain will have soaked in.

Low-lying areas where flooding could or is known to be a problem should be planned for. Try to ensure all soil is covered with plants or grass to reduce erosion and possible extensive soil loss, including any nutrients.

There are a number of other techniques that can be used to reduce flooding that require changes to the design of the garden. These techniques are not extensive or expensive and can be carried out by the home gardener; they include bioswales, rain gardens, dew ponds and natural ponds.

Bioswales and Swales

These are long, shallow, round-based ditches that control the flow of water and hold it temporarily, allowing it to soak into the ground. They are more widely used in the USA, adjacent to car parks, roads and other large impermeable surfaces. The base and sides of the swale are planted up with vigorous plants that can use the water and help slow the flow. The length and width will depend on the space available and how much water is likely to enter it.

Swales are useful if the ground naturally slopes – even if only slightly. Instead of allowing the water to flow straight down the slope and gather speed and quantity, the swale slows the water and holds it for a time. If possible, design the swale so it flows slightly across but still down the slope. This spreads the water over a wider area and slows the flow even more, allowing it to soak into the soil. As the water is spread over a wider area it allows more plants to make use of it, saving on future irrigation.

Bioswales can be grassed over and mown, left long with wildflowers or planted up with groundcover or other low plants. They can be attractive features in their own right, especially if flowering plants are used. The plants help to slow the flow of water and use some of it.

The swale can end at a pond, pool, bog garden or drain, or just act as a dead end to hold the water until it soaks into the soil. Some large swales have a storm drain at the end to take the remaining water; if this is the case, have this protruding from the ground so that it does not come into use until the swale is full of water.

Ponds

A natural pond in low areas will hold and store water away from more important areas of the garden and forms a very good habitat for a wide range of creatures, from insects and birds to reptiles. The size of the pond will need to be in scale with the rest of the garden and may fluctuate over the year, being large in the winter and smaller during dry periods in the summer (in fact, some may dry up over the summer). The larger the better, as bigger ponds hold more water and reduce the likelihood of flooding or damage to other parts of the garden. The pond could be dug out using machinery, or if there is a natural depression just allow this to fill up with water.

If a pond is not a possibility but ditches are available, water can be guided or diverted to the ditch. Try to avoid large amounts of water entering the ditch in a short period of time as this can result in flooding further downstream. Ensure the water is not directed towards other properties, causing damage. If the ditch flows into a stream or river, permission may be required from the Environment Agency or Scottish equivalent for directing water into the ditch.

Plant Adaptations

Plants have adapted to living in wet conditions in a couple of ways. Firstly, they produce a tissue called aerenchyma, which has a high number of air spaces, usually in the stems. The plant can then transport oxygen from the leaves via the stems to its roots. Most plants cannot do this – they can move water and solutes but not gases like oxygen. Secondly, they use anaerobic instead of aerobic respiration, however this is less efficient and produces considerably less energy from the carbohydrate produced by photosynthesis. It also produces ethanol or alcohol, which can be toxic to plants.

Choosing flood-tolerant plants is not easy, but consider the natural habitat the plant grows in, for example the edges of ponds, lakes, rivers, or streams, as well as marsh and bog areas. These areas will likely to be wet and prone to flooding, so the plants will have evolved to grow in these conditions.

Wet Gardens

Very few plants will grow in permanently saturated soil – bog plants and some aquatic plants being the exception, as they have evolved and adapted to grow in such conditions. If the soil is likely to be wet for long periods, the options are rather limited.

Firstly, you can choose plants that have adapted to these conditions, like the above plant types. Secondly, install a drainage system, although this can be expensive and needs an outlet into a stream, ditch or large soakaway. Thirdly, you can install a number of raised beds that raise the soil above the level of the wet soil. Raised beds can be expensive as they need a large amount of soil (unless they are small), however they are useful for vegetable growing and can, with careful design, be incorporated into an attractive garden design by blending them into the area.

Wet soils tend to need more maintenance, owing to there being more weeds germinating and making more growth than in a dry soil. Hoeing is less successful as a method of weed control as the weeds will often re-root into the wet soil after being hoed off; the weeds should be raked up and composted. If the soil is fairly wet, weeds are better removed by hand, weeding and forking out at regular intervals and before they flower and seed – weekly or every ten days during the peak growing period of late April to early July. Many cultivated plants usually make more growth in damp or wet soils as they are rarely short of water and the soils can often be fertile – this can mean more pruning, deadheading and other plant maintenance. Conversely, wet soils usually need less watering during dry periods than dry or sandy soils. This will be an advantage during the likely frequent droughts in the future.

During the winter, it is important to keep off wet soils as it results in compaction and damage to the soil structure. Compacted soils drain less well, as the water cannot pass through them easily and less oxygen is available for root respiration, which can inhibit growth. Poorly structured soils are difficult for the roots to penetrate and therefore grow. They also tend to have poorer drainage and aeration, usually resulting in poor plant growth and stressed plants prone to pest and disease attack. If it is really necessary to go onto the soil, work off long planks that spread your weight over a wider area, causing less compaction.

In the future, rather than severe cold or frost damage, it is more likely to be the increasingly wet soil conditions that result in plant death owing to the roots or plants rotting. It will be important to ensure the soil is as free draining as possible or the plants have adapted to wet conditions. Water – either the lack or excess of it – is likely to be a big problem in the future. We may need to reduce the amount of water that plants receive by adding simple covers like cloches, improving the drainage, or where possible diverting water away from borders towards other areas.

Keeping the soil covered by layers of plant foliage will help to reduce the amount of rainfall that goes into the soil and slow the speed of water entering the soil. The use of groundcover plants with other plants like trees or shrubs above not only protects the soil but also gives a three-dimensional effect that forms a more attractive garden, usually adding colour and interest.

SOIL EROSION CONTROL

Soil erosion is more of a problem on farmers' fields and open spaces, but if you have a sloping garden or live near a watercourse, it could occur. It would be wise to take some form of precaution as once soil erosion has occurred it is too late and you have lost your soil, leaving just the low-fertile subsoil and resulting in poor plant growth.

Having a watercourse running through or at the bottom of the garden may be idyllic for most of the year. However, if the water levels rise quickly, it can start to erode the banks and part of your garden by flooding over into the garden, taking topsoil with it. There is likely nothing you can do about the water levels as this is owing to the weather and water coming from further upstream. What you *can* do is to support and reinforce the banks with faggots, which are widely used by the Environment Agency on rivers and streams. A faggot is a tied-up bundle of prunings or small branches, often freely available near watercourses, which are pinned into place with wooden stakes to prevent the water washing them away.

An alternative to using faggots is to use willow or poplar rods along watercourses. These are very large cuttings – from 50cm (20in) to 2m (6½ft) long, depending on the depth of the bank and water – that are either pushed or hammered into the soil. They quickly take root, which holds the soil in place and reduces erosion. They can also quickly form a screen, which can be trimmed to a suitable height; just prune them back annually to maintain their width and height.

It also pays to avoid having bare earth adjacent to a watercourse as the soil is easily washed away; it is useful to have trees or shrubs growing, as their roots help to hold the bank in position.

If you have sloping ground, is it possible to reduce the degree of the slope or construct terracing to prevent water picking up speed and taking the soil with it? Placing barriers in the way will help to slow the water and catch some of the soil. Keeping the soil covered with layers of plants prevents erosion, as will a good grass cover. Some plants with good root systems to hold the soil are willows such as *Salix alba* 'Britzensis', *Salix hastata* 'Wehrhahnii' and *Salix lanata*, poplars, *Cornus sericea*, *Sambucus racemosa* 'Plumosa Aurea' and *Sambucus nigra* 'Black Lace Eva'.

Swales can be constructed for a larger area, which guide the water slowly across the slope and allow it to soak into the ground. These could end in a pond or depression to catch the water like a rain garden. If the swale has a very gradual decline, much of the water will soak into the soil before it reaches the bottom. If space allows, a series of swales can be constructed.

On steep slopes, gabions can be used to form terraces and reduce the slope. These can be filled with stone, hardcore or other heavy waste. They can be made onsite or delivered and craned in, put in place and linked together to hold them in position. It is possible to have climbers or other plants growing over them if they look unsightly.

Composting

Composting is not only an important part of gardening but also helps in reducing climate change, as all compost added to the soil will be adding carbon, as well as some nutrients needed for plant growth. Compost recycles green waste material such as weeds, grass cuttings, thin prunings, green kitchen waste, crop and other plant remains, as well as paper and cardboard. Compost can be incorporated into the soil, used as a mulch and, if sieved, used in containers. It improves soil fertility, increases water and nutrient holding, feeds soil fauna and improves soil structure on any soil. You will never have too much compost and should make as much as possible.

Compost is best if made in a bin as this holds the material together and helps to keep it moist and hold the heat. Bins of $1m^3$ ($3\frac{1}{4}ft^3$) or larger produce the best compost; smaller bins will not work quite as well. The bins can be made from wood, brick, blocks, metal, second-hand sleepers, straw bales, or anything that can be constructed to hold in plant waste. Build them on soil and in a partly shaded position (although they will still work in full sun or shade). Many books give various ways to build a compost heap, but to keep it simple just add the waste material in layers as it becomes available. Try to have a 50/50 mix of green and brown materials.

Compost heaps – all green waste should be composted to produce a very good source of organic matter, which can be used to improve soils or as a mulch. This makes good use of green waste.

Leaf mould heap – leaves raked up in the autumn, stacked in a wire mesh frame and left for a year or two to rot form a very good soil improver.

Green Materials

- Grass cuttings
- Young weeds
- Kitchen peelings
- Any soft plant growth

Brown Materials

- Prunings
- Cardboard or newspaper
- Cabbage stalks
- Other thick stems
- Woodchips or sawdust

The thicker the layers added, the quicker they warm up and the higher the temperature achieved. The aim is for 60–70°C as this kills any pests, diseases and weed seeds. Lower temperatures are fine, but just allow for the fact there is likely to be weed seeds in the compost if you have added flowering weeds to the heap. Keep the compost heap covered with a piece of carpet or sheet of polythene to prevent too much rain entering and help to retain the heat from decomposing.

Trench Composting

This is useful if you have no space for a compost bin or do not wish to have one, as it still allows you to make good use of waste organic matter. It is also useful in dry areas as it gets a large amount of organic matter into a small area of soil.

Dig out a trench one to two spades wide and at least one spade deep and place the soil to one side, out of the way. If the soil is compacted at the bottom of the trench it can be forked over, like double digging. Any organic waste is added to the trench – add coarse material like sweetcorn and brassica stems to the bottom and smaller material to the top until it is full and then replace the soil. The ground will now be higher than it was, but will settle back nearly to its previous level as the organic matter decomposes.

Trench composting can be carried out at any time of the year but is usually done in the winter. It is an old-fashioned technique that was used where runner beans were to be grown. The advantages of trench composting are there is no turning – or if you wish to turn the compost, it will be a lot easier. There is no need to barrow the compost to the site as it's already there, and it also produces a deep fertile soil.

Green Manure

I could write a whole chapter on green manure, but as that is not the purpose of this book I will restrict it to a section in this chapter. Green manure – or cover crops, as the Americans call them – have been increasing in use over the last thirty years and are more widely grown than they used to be. Having said that, even more should be grown, especially as the effects of climate change increase, as they have a number of advantages to the soil and environment.

Green manures are a good method of adding organic matter to the soil, especially if you do not have access to manure or other sources of organic matter. With the right choice of plants, green manure will grow for most of the year so they make good use of the land. A winter crop of green manure will not only add organic matter to the soil but will also protect the surface soil from capping during heavy rain

Mustard green manure – a common plant used as a green manure sown in late summer/early autumn and then incorporated into the soil or composted.

Buckwheat – a summer-grown green manure that is quick growing and produces a large amount of material to add to the soil.

(more likely owing to climate change). It also prevents the leaching of nutrients by that rain. This is partly owing to the protection given by the plants' foliage and also the plant takes up the nutrients and recycles them when dug in. Green manure plants also absorb CO_2 and when the plant is incorporated into the soil, this carbon is sequestered into the soil.

Some deep-rooted plants will help to break up compacted soils and bring nutrients up from the lower soil levels. These are returned to the soil within reach of plants and crops when the green manure is dug in.

There are now a wide range of green manure plants available including mustard, *Phacelia*, ryegrasses, fenugreek, clovers, vetch, field beans and more. One plant I have seen recommended for drought and hot conditions is Sudan grass (*Sorghum* spp.) – this may be worth considering for summer growing during dry periods when many other plants will not grow.

It is important as the effects of climate change get worse that we both protect the soil from heavy rain and excessive heat and improve the organic matter and carbon level of the soils. Whenever the soil is not being used, sow a green manure crop and incorporate into the soil two to three weeks before sowing or planting.

Alfalfa green manure – a nitrogen fixer and very drought-tolerant plant that can be cut down two or three times a year for composting.

Undersowing

This is a fairly recent technique, which involves the sowing of a second crop under the main crop. This makes efficient use of the land; very important in these days of land shortage, which will only get worse in the future. The main crop can be vegetables like sweetcorn, runner and French beans, or Brassica (like cabbage, Brussels sprouts, calabrese or broccoli); all these crops are widely spaced, leaving plenty of space for other plants, including weeds! The aim is to sow a lower-growing plant, like clovers or similar low-growing green manures, which grow but do not compete too much with the main crop. Once the main crop is harvested, the under crop can be cut and composted, dug in or mown off and allowed to regrow, digging it in at a later date or planting another taller crop.

Undersowing makes efficient use of the land, recycles nutrients, improves the soil when incorporated,

Low-growing Green Manures, Suitable for Undersowing

- *Lotus corniculatus* (Bird's foot trefoil) – grows approximately 20–30cm (8–12in) high. A good weed suppressor and fixes nitrogen; mainly grown over the summer but is hardy enough to overwinter.
- *Medicago lupulina* (Yellow trefoil) – a low-growing, short-lived plant; will self-seed if left after flowering.
- *Trifolium pratense* (Red clover) – more vigorous than white clover; fixes nitrogen and attracts bees.
- *Trifolium incarnatum* (Crimson clover) – an annual that can be used to give a quick crop of green manure.
- *Trifolium repens* (White clover) – a reasonably quick-growing plant, grows to 20–30cm (8–12in) high. Often seen as a weed in lawns; its flowers attract bees.

helps to reduce weed growth, adds carbon to the soil and – if a legume is grown – will add nitrogen to the soil as well.

Improving the Soil Carbon Sink

We can all do our bit to reduce the amount of carbon dioxide in the atmosphere by sequestering carbon into the soil and growing as many plants as possible in our gardens, as all plants absorb CO_2. The soil holds four times the amount of carbon than is stored in the atmosphere, and more than all the plants in the world, and it is important that this carbon stays in the soil and we sequester more into it.

The aim is to produce a deep, fertile, rich soil with a high level of carbon stored within it. Any plant material added will add carbon, which as it decomposes is locked into the soil.

Factors to Help Improve the Soil Carbon Sink

- Convert to no-dig or use minimum cultivations.
- Avoid walking over the soil where possible, as this compacts it.
- Use permanent plantings including herbaceous perennials, shrubs and trees, as these lock up more carbon than annuals.
- Avoid bare soil surfaces by covering with groundcover plants, green manure or a mulch. Fill any gaps in borders with annuals or groundcover plants.
- Improve the soil by adding organic matter, green manure or ramial woodchip and undersow any wide-spacing crops.

CHAPTER 3

LAWNS AND WILDFLOWER MEADOWS

Do we need to rethink having verdant green lawns in most of the UK; are they a thing of the past with climate change? To keep a lawn green over dry summer periods needs an exorbitant amount of water that we can ill afford and cannot be justified, except for some sports turf areas. We may need to accept that green lawns are possible for eight or nine months of the year but we must either allow them to go brown during the height of the summer or remove them. If retained they can then be renovated in the autumn, or just allowed to recover over the winter – which most will do – and, if required, renovated in the spring.

An alternative is to look at other options if summers are regularly going to be hot and dry. We need to avoid any hard landscaping, as this will just create increased chances of flooding and higher temperatures. A low-maintenance option is an area of raked gravel or sand, as seen in Japanese gardens, which are tidy and can include water, plants or rocks to provide interest. They just require regular raking to create a pattern in the gravel or sand. Other alternatives to lawns are discussed later in this chapter and include wildflower areas, herb lawns and other planting.

Small lawns or grass areas can be maintained using hand equipment (push mowers), so have a very low carbon footprint, but larger areas need powered machinery and, if mown regularly to maintain a reasonable standard, have a higher carbon footprint. This is definitely the case if fertiliser is applied, and the lawn is scarified and aerated by machinery to maintain a high-quality lawn. Lawn fertilisers are high in nitrogen, and this requires a lot of energy to produce.

Good lawns can be very time-consuming to maintain to a good standard: they can require up to three applications of fertiliser, an annual herbicide spray or treatment, scarifying, aerating and top dressing. Although they will absorb some CO_2, they have a very low diversity as there is only the grass plants and no flowering plants if weeds have been sprayed to remove them. If the grass is irrigated to keep it green in the summer, this can use a considerable amount of water over a drought period.

On the plus side, good lawns look attractive and set off the rest of the garden, are a good permeable surface to absorb rainwater, and provide a habitat for some insects. If not maintained to too high a standard and as much work as possible is done by hand, they will not have too high a carbon footprint. Gardeners have come to accept they should have a lawn as part of their overall garden design, and many gardens have a lawn of some kind. We need to change our thinking about lawns and lawn maintenance now that climate change is starting to have an effect.

Crocus growing in grass, giving good spring colour. After flowering, they are left to die back naturally and the area is not mown until the foliage has gone brown.

A drought-affected lawn. Most of the grass has gone brown but it had mainly recovered by mid-October.

LAWN MAINTENANCE

Conventional lawn maintenance requires a lot of mowing and fertiliser use so is not very sustainable, especially if powered mowers are used – whether they are petrol, diesel, electric or battery, they are using energy. Lawns are not a good habitat for a biodiverse population of creatures.

To create a more biodiverse lawn, first stop applying herbicides and fertilisers. Next reduce the frequency of mowing to once a fortnight, or longer if possible, and raise the height of cut of the mower blades to 5cm (2in) or higher. The higher the height of cut, the greater the range of plants that will grow in the lawn. If mown at fortnightly intervals at 5cm (2in) high, the lawn is still suitable for children to play on or for alfresco picnicking and you will get daisies, dandelions, clovers, mouse-eared chickweed, selfheal, speedwell, black medic and more growing and flowering. Bulbs could be planted to give early colour if wanted: crocus, winter aconite and snowdrop would all grow in these conditions.

Reducing the mowing frequency not only saves energy but also the cost of fuel, which has increased dramatically in recent years. The frequency will depend on the types of grasses in the lawn; if they are coarse grasses or ryegrass they will need mowing every two to three weeks but for a bent/fescue mix, once a month will be ample.

Autumn Lawn Renovation

If you wish to continue to have a mown lawn and accept that it will go brown during the summer, it will need renovating each autumn, which should mean it will be green for about eight months of the year. Wait until the autumn rains arrive (or at least until we have had a few showers to soften the ground) and start to green up the grass. Unless you are happy with a few wildflowers (weeds!), remove these by hand or using a selective weedkiller.

Heavily rake or scarify by hand or machine to remove as much dead material as possible – this can all be composted. Providing the ground is not too hard, spike the lawn with a fork or machine to improve the soil aeration and allow water penetration. Follow this by overseeding at approximately 17g (½oz) per 1m² (3½ft²) with the grasses you want to encourage. Finally, top dress the lawn with a soil/sand or soil/leaf mould (or similar mix) at 2–5kg (4½–11lb) per 1m² (3½ft²) and brush or lute this into the lawn surface.

If it is not too late in the growing season, an autumn fertiliser can be applied, but do not apply a spring/summer feed as these are too high in nitrogen and can encourage disease at this time of the year. After this treatment, the lawn may look battered for three weeks or so, but soon greens up and grows and will look healthy until the next drought. If when over-seeding drought-tolerant grasses are used over a period of years, you will develop a more drought-tolerant lawn.

Drought-tolerant Lawns

Raising the height of cut to 5cm (2in) will encourage the lower-growing weeds and wildflowers, but if the height is raised to 10cm (4in) or even 20cm (8in) a wider range of wildflowers will grow, including daisies, dandelions, clovers, birds-foot trefoil, speedwell, plantain, selfheal, buttercups, cat's ear, celandine, mouse-eared chickweed, yarrow and many others. Which species grow will depend on the soil type and pH, what is in the soil weed seed bank and what is growing locally for the seed to blow in or be deposited by birds.

It is important when mowing or strimming to remove grass clippings to help reduce the fertility of the soil: the poorer the soil fertility, the wider the range of wildflowers and the better they are able to compete with the grasses. Soils with lower fertility help to restrain the coarse and vigorous grasses. This can be encouraged by sowing yellow rattle (*Rhinanthus minor*), which parasitises the grass plants, reducing their growth. The collected grass cuttings should be put on the compost heap as they will make good compost and speed up the composting process.

This type of lawn will not require watering as both the grasses and wildflowers develop a deeper root system than mown lawns and will recover or produce seed that will grow after the drought period. Most wildflowers are also fairly flood tolerant, as long as the flood does not last too long. If the area is regularly waterlogged, choose species of plants that have evolved to grow in such conditions.

ALTERNATIVE LAWNS

What are the alternatives to grass lawns? Plastic grass may be the first thought, but this is not sustainable, does not allow much rainwater percolation, does not absorb CO_2 or provide a habitat for wildlife, so should be avoided.

There are some species and cultivars of grasses that make very little growth in a year, so only need cutting twice a year to keep the lawn neat and tidy. These lawns do not require much maintenance and often work well with wildflowers, as they do not compete with them. The downside is that they do not tolerate heavy wear, so cannot be used for playing or sports.

Instead of grasses for a lawn, there are alternative plants that not only require less mowing but some will flower, thus providing pollen and nectar for bees and other pollinators. Some have scented leaves and others coloured leaves, which provides a change to green. They can be walked on (but not regularly or for use as a footpath) and sat on, but they do not provide a surface suitable for play.

Alternative Plants for Lawns

Chamomile

Chamomile has been used as a substitute lawn for many years, although it is not that widely used and deserves to be used more. Chamomile is a low-growing aromatic herb, which can be walked on – but not too regularly – and is fairly drought tolerant. The cultivar 'Treneague' forms a good alternative to grass for lawns.

Clovers and Microclovers

There are several clovers available, some of which are used for green manures and these would be too tall and vigorous for a clover lawn. Clovers are useful on poor soils, even subsoils and clay soils. They not only flower for a long period in the summer, but also fix nitrogen from the air and convert it into a form used by plants. When the clover roots die off, the nitrogen is available to the next plants. A reasonably low-growing clover is the white clover (*Trifolium repens*); this may need mowing if it gets too tall and cutting back at the edges or it can spread into the borders.

Microclovers were bred from the white clovers often seen in lawns and other grass areas, and were developed in Holland and Denmark for use on golf courses. They will give a lush green colour, even in drought conditions, without any irrigation. They do not require a lot of maintenance – possibly just two mows a year, no feeding, and can be walked on like a lawn. However, they are not as hard-wearing as some grasses, so are best not used on areas of heavy wear.

Microclovers are miniature strains of the white clover. Its leaves are about a third of the size of the white clover and it is about half the height. It is slow growing and does not produce many flowers (so not ideal for pollinators). It can be used on its own for a 100 per cent microclover lawn or mixed with grasses to give a blended effect. Microclovers can be sown from scratch, oversown into an existing lawn, or sown as a mix of grass and clover.

Preparation for a new microclover lawn is the same as for a grass lawn: fork the area over, break up any lumps, firm the area and rake a tilth. As microclover seed is very small, it is important to rake a fine crumbly tilth, sow the seed by broadcasting over the area and rake it into the soil. New lawns are sown at 5–7g per 1m² (3¼ft²) and can be sown in the spring or autumn. If overseeding an existing lawn, sow at 3–5g per 1m² (3¼ft²) and if sowing a mixed grass/clover lawn, the clover should be 2–3 per cent of the mix.

A couple of microclover cultivars available are 'Euromic' and 'Jura'. 'Euromic' is dwarf, only growing up to 15cm (6in) and producing few flowers; it can be mown to a lower height if required. 'Jura' is slightly taller, at up to 20cm (8in) if not mown (lower if mown). It does not require any irrigation, even in dry conditions, and will stay green all year round. Sow in early spring or late autumn at 2g per 1m² (3¼ft²) for overseeding and 5–10g per 1m² (3¼ft²) for a full clover lawn.

If sowing as part of a clover/grass mix, up to 5 per cent can be clover. Pipolina is a dark green microclover, which can be added to grass seed at 5 per cent clover to grass seed. It is drought- and salt-tolerant so can be used near the sea or alongside salt-treated roads, and it can be close mown. One disadvantage of both clover and microclover lawns is they cannot be treated with selective lawn weedkillers to kill other plants as this will kill the clover as well.

Acaena microphylla

This is a native of New Zealand with small grey-green to bronze leaves and very small flowers that are

Acaena microphylla 'Kupferteppich' – a very low-growing plant, suitable for a non-grass lawn.

followed by red burrs, giving a long period of interest. It is evergreen and grows to 3cm (1¼in) height. There is a cultivar called 'Kupferteppich', and one called Acaena 'Blue Haze' that is taller at 8cm high and has blue-grey foliage. They will grow on poor soils and require little maintenance other than an annual tidy-up in the autumn by clipping it back or running over it with a sharp-bladed rotary mower.

Thymes

Thymes are low-growing subshrubs and herbs that are drought-tolerant, grow on poor soils and, in fact, are more highly scented on a poorer soil. Most will flower and attract bees and other insects. Maintenance involves an annual clip after flowering to remove the old flower heads and encourage fresh new growth – use shears or a sharp rotary mower. There are many thymes available with different coloured leaves and scents; they can be planted as a single colour or you can create a patchwork effect.

Useful and Easily Available Thymes

- *Thymus* 'Silver Queen' – a variegated form of lemon thyme that has pink flowers in the summer.
- *Thymus* × *citriodorus* – lemon thyme with pink flowers.
- *Thymus* × *citriodorus* 'Variegata' – a variegated form of lemon thyme.
- *Thymus pulegioides* – a common form with dark green leaves and purplish flowers.
- *Thymus pulegioides* 'Bertram Anderson' – a good golden form.
- *Thymus nitidus* 'Peter Davis' – grey-green leaves and pink flowers.
- *Thymus citriodorus* 'Archer's Gold' – light green with a hint of yellow.

Thymus citriodorus 'Archer's Gold' – one of the thymes used for non-grass lawns. It gives a nice yellow sheen to the area, as well as being scented when walked on.

Leptinella squalida

Also called *Cotula squalida*, this is another very low-growing plant from New Zealand. It flowers to add further interest, but can be invasive so needs cutting back each spring to prevent it spreading. There are green-leaved and almost black-leaved types available. It is evergreen and grows to approximately 3cm (1¼in) high.

Mentha requienii

A very low-growing mint with a nice scent. It will tolerate some shade, but again will need cutting back to prevent it spreading.

Soleirolia soleirolii

Also known as 'mind your own business', this is very low growing – as low as 5cm (2in). It will grow in shade and damp soil but, a word of warning, it can be invasive!

There are many other low-growing plants suitable for alternative lawns; have a look in nurseries, online or in garden centres for suitable plants.

Moss

Many gardeners spend a lot of time, effort and money trying to get rid of moss from both lawns and paved areas, yet if it is so successful why not make use of it? There are thousands of species of moss, and the right ones will need selecting to produce a good substitute lawn. Mosses are not very drought resistant but will, like grass, grow back once the rains come.

Moss is widely used in Japanese gardens and fits in with their design. It is very low growing and requires minimum maintenance as no mowing nor fertiliser is required. Many species grow well in shade and others will tolerate very acid or alkaline soils, although most prefer damp conditions, but it is likely there will be a species to suit your conditions.

Moss is very expensive to buy, but if it grows naturally on your soils and the area you wish to have a moss lawn, just encourage it to grow. It prefers damp and shady areas but will recover in the autumn after a hot dry summer, and on my lawn seems to recover more quickly and better than the grasses!

Possible Moss Options

- Hypnales
- Haircap – *Polytrichum commune* and *P. formosum*
- Thyme mosses – *Mnium hornum*
- Tamarisk moss – *Thuidium tamariscinum* and *T. delicatulum*
- Greater fork moss – *Dicranum majus*

Slow- and Low-growing Grasses

These grasses were first developed in the 1970s but never became widely used – had they been used more; it would have saved a lot of time and mower fuel! These are a mix of slow-growing grass species that do not grow too tall, so require little mowing – in fact, as little as one to four mows per year is sufficient to maintain an attractive lawn. If a short lawn is required, it will need mowing four times a year; but if a longer lawn of, say, 10cm (4in) is satisfactory, one or two mows will keep it tidy. As well as little mowing, the grasses will tolerate poor, dry soils and some shade, so will be suitable for many gardens and will produce a sustainable lawn. Different companies have slightly different mixtures, but the mix below is a reliable all-fescue one, which gives a lawn of fine grasses.

- 25 per cent Chewings fescue
- 60 per cent Strong creeping fescue
- 5 per cent Slender creeping fescue
- 7 per cent Hard fescue
- 3 per cent Sheep's fescue

Sow the above at 35g (1¼oz) per 1m² (3¼ft²).

For a slightly longer lawn that still requires little mowing, the following mixture is more widely available and still slow growing:

- 25 per cent Barkoel crested hairgrass
- 20 per cent Hardtop hard fescue
- 35 per cent Barpearl slender creeping red fescue
- 20 per cent Bargreen Chewings fescue

If you want to reduce your mowing time or do not like mowing, give these grasses a go.

Wildflower Lawns

In recent times, flower meadows have become popular not only with gardeners but many local authorities have also established them on roundabouts and grass verges because they look attractive, are good for wildlife and also reduce the mowing required. They can look a bit scruffy once flowering has finished, but they can then be mown and cleared.

Flower meadows provide flowers for pollinators and other insects and a habitat for greater biodiversity. They also have a reduced carbon footprint compared to a conventional lawn. They require less mowing but need from two to four cuts a year, depending on the species of plants in them. Mowing also prevents the area turning to scrub vegetation over time.

There are three main methods of creating a flower meadow or wildflower area. The first is to start from scratch and sow seeds; the second is to buy in or grow plug plants or seedlings and plant the area often into existing grass; and the third is to allow the existing lawn to convert to a wildflower area by lifting the height of cut on the mower and reducing the frequency of mowing.

Try a 'No Mow May' and see what plants (weeds!) grow. The most common are daisies, dandelions, clover, speedwell, pearlwort, plantains and buttercups. These all flower and add interest and colour to the lawn. If required, once they are established they could be supplemented by adding plug plants of additional species in the spring or late autumn.

Meadow mix display – a narrow area sown with a meadow mix. Rather than a grass verge, this gives a far more colourful display and provides many flowers for pollinators.

Wildflowers in a natural setting give a good summer display and will be mown in September, once flowering is complete.

If a wildflower area of a certain range of species is required, these can be grown or purchased as plug plants and planted in the lawn or bare soil. Mow the lawn as short as possible and then plant the plug plants directly into the lawn. It helps them establish if a square of turf approximately 20cm (8in) is scraped off with a spade first, as this reduces the competition for the plug plants. Do not make the planting hole too small and push the plants in; a larger hole with some loose soil gives better establishment. Place the plant in position and firm the plants in then water.

Once planted, allow the grass to grow and the plants to establish, and water if it is a dry spring. Mow the lawn with the blades set above the plug plant height to control the grasses; after the initial cut, mow at the frequency recommended for the plants being grown.

Starting from scratch involves the most work but usually gives the best results. Some wildflower areas are just sown once and will last for years; others are resown each year. This is affected by the type and choice of plants; the more floriferous flower meadows are resown each year to ensure a good show of colourful flowers.

Wildflower meadows are ideal for people just moving into a newly built home as the builders have usually trashed (or sold) the soil, leaving a poor-quality subsoil and rubble mix. Poor soils are ideal for most wildflowers and there is no need to add any soil improvement materials. Note the type of soil (sandy or clay), and if possible check the pH (whether it is acid or alkaline) as these affect the choice of plants, although many plants are not too fussy.

Remove any builders' rubbish in the top 15cm (6in) and either use as hardcore under paths, drives or patios or bury it under the meadow. If the soil is a clay, the hardcore could be used to make a soakaway to help with drainage. This saves disposal costs and has a low carbon footprint.

Grade the soil to the levels required and either fork over – removing any perennial weeds – and break up any lumps, or rotary cultivate the area. Rake the soil level to a fine tilth, firm it slightly by treading and re-rake. Then sow the seed by broadcasting evenly, and rake the seed into the soil. As wildflower and meadow seed is expensive, sow it carefully to ensure you cover the whole area. It can help to mix the seed with dry sand to give an even distribution and spread. If birds or cats are likely to be a problem, cover the area with fleece or place some sticks around the area and string cotton over to deter them. When the seed has

Annual meadow or pictorial mix, giving a bright show of colour. These can be resown each year to keep them fresh and ensure a good display.

germinated, check whether it needs cutting – many flower meadow mixtures do not.

If the area to be a wildflower meadow has a good fertile soil, this is best removed and used to make raised beds in the vegetable garden or spread on borders elsewhere in the garden. The wildflowers are sown into the poorer subsoil, which gives a better flower display and less competition from vigorous grasses.

To add a bit of interest to wildflower meadows, paths can be mown through them. This allows you to get close to the plants, and a ring mown around the perimeter helps to show the area is maintained and not a rough, unkempt area. Most meadows need mowing at the end of the season (September/October) when the spent growth is cut down and removed. The mowings can be left for a few days for any seed to drop onto the soil to grow next year. After that, either rake up the remains or pick up with a mower and put on the compost heap. If the cuttings are not removed, they decompose and are incorporated by worms, which improves the soil, and this tends to encourage the coarser rougher grasses, not wildflowers.

Trifolium repens (white clover) – a useful plant as it has a long flowering period and makes its own nitrogen, being a legume. A good plant for pollinating insects, especially bees.

Wildflower and annual mix, giving a range of plants and colour. The plants can be changed each year to give new interest.

The main flower in this mix is ox-eye daisy; other flowers have finished and will self-seed in the area.

Types of Wildflowers

- Bird's foot trefoil – *Lotus corniculatus*
- Black medick – *Medicago lupulina*
- Buttercups – *Ranunculus* species
- Campion – *Silene* species
- Cat's ear – *Hypochaeris radicata*
- Cinquefoils – *Potentilla* species
- Clovers – *Trifolium* species
- Coltsfoot – *Tussilago farfara*
- Corncockle – *Agrostemma githago*
- Cornflower – *Centaurea cyanus*
- Corn marigold – *Chrysanthemum segetum*
- Cowslip – *Primula veris*
- Field poppy – *Papaver rhoeas*
- Field scabious – *Knautia arvensis*
- Hawkweed – *Hieracium* species
- Heart's ease – *Viola tricolor*
- Knapweeds – *Centaurea scabiosa*
- Meadow crane's-bill – *Geranium pratense*
- Plantains – *Plantago* species
- Primrose – *Primula vulgaris*
- Ox-eye daisy – *Leucanthemum vulgare*
- Salad burnet – *Sanguisorba minor*
- Selfheal – *Prunella vulgaris*
- Stitchwort – *Stellaria holostea*
- Yellow toadflax – *Linaria vulgaris*

Successful Flower Meadow Plants

- *Amaranthus cruentus*
- *Ammi majus*
- *Calendula officinalis*
- *Dimorphotheca aurantiaca*
- *Eschscholzia californica*
- *Helianthus annuus*
- *Limnanthes douglasii*
- *Linaria purpurea*
- *Lunaria annua*
- *Moluccella laevis*
- *Nigella damascena*
- *Papaver nudicaule*
- *Salvia horminum*

The amount of colour in the meadow can be increased by adding hardy annuals to the mixture and some meadow mixes already do this. This is fine but not always acceptable to purists as not all hardy annuals are native plants.

Hardy annuals can be sown in the spring when the soil is moist and just warming up. They usually make rapid growth, starting to flower from June through to September. If the soil becomes very dry, they will die, but they can just be raked or mown off and resown the next year – there is no big loss as they are cheap to buy and still put on a good show of colour. Some will have self-seeded and will germinate in the autumn and flower earlier next year, beating any hot weather.

Drought-tolerant Lawns

Some species of grass are more drought tolerant than others. The most common grass used for British lawns is ryegrass (*Lolium perenne*). This is a resilient grass, highly suitable for the British climate up until recent years. It will thrive in moist, mild weather, typical of the winters and sometimes summers in the UK, but is not adapted to hot conditions or spells of dry weather and drought conditions. For a grass it has a reasonably broad leaf and is relatively quick-growing, so needs a good amount of water to thrive. It tends to go brown in dry summers, although it will recover once the rains return. If it is important to maintain a green appearance on the lawn – and I would argue in most cases, it is not – then choose drought-tolerant grasses.

The first of these grasses is *Festuca arundinacea* (a type of sheep's fescue, also called a rhizomatous tall fescue), which is very good in drought conditions and also tolerates both cold and waterlogged conditions. This grass has a very good, deep root system that gets down to moisture well below the capability of other grasses – this is the reason it is drought tolerant. Its other advantage is that it has a rolled leaf where the grass blade rolls into a cylinder with the stomata on the inside. This reduces water loss quite considerably; therefore it has a lower water requirement than other grasses.

The other grass with good drought tolerance is *Poa pratensis* (also called smooth stalked meadow grass and, in America, Kentucky blue grass). This has a good root system. It tends to go dormant during hot weather and quickly regrows when the rains arrive.

A mix of these two grasses should give a good lawn that will survive most droughts and recover fairly quickly. They should not be cut too short, especially during the summer, and will usually maintain a light green colour in hot, dry periods.

The days of the UK having verdant green lawns could be over as climate change progresses, so we need to decide what to grow in their place. Hopefully the above has given you some options to consider.

CHAPTER 4

WATER USE AND IRRIGATION

After sunlight and soil, water is the most valuable natural resource available to the gardener. Without water, plants will not grow; although too much water will result in the plants' death. We do not at present have any control over rainfall and this is unlikely to change in the short term. One of the effects of climate change is that rainfall has become inconsistent, with heavier rain for longer periods of time followed by prolonged periods without any rain. In the southeast of the UK, we are getting less rain in the spring and summer but more in late autumn and winter. At times, this can be excessive, resulting in flooding and waterlogging of the soils. As individuals, we are unlikely to be able to control major flooding – this is a role for the Environment Agency and local and national governments – but we can control how much water leaves our property, adding to flooding further downstream.

PREVENTING WATER LOSS

It is as important to prevent water loss as it is to prevent flooding if plants are to grow healthily. We need to make maximum use of available water, if only to reduce our use of tap water in the garden, which is an expensive use of a valuable water supply. Tap water has had expensive treatments and energy has been used to

pump it along the pipes – its use in the garden is not sustainable.

When it rains it either falls on the soil and percolates into it, or if the soil is already waterlogged it will run off, causing flooding. Otherwise, rain lands on buildings, hard landscaped areas and roads; much of which runs down the drains and is lost and wasted. We need to harvest and store more rainwater for use in the garden and possibly for flushing toilets and other uses where chlorinated tap water is not essential. It would also help if hard surfaces like drives were permeable to allow water into the ground rather than running off, causing flooding elsewhere. As the weather becomes more unpredictable, we need to be ready to collect more rain when it does occur.

Watering Plants

When choosing plants for our gardens, we should select those that have a low requirement for water and will survive without any watering – these are covered in the Plant Directory (see Chapter 8). Try to group plants that have similar requirements together so that water can be used efficiently. Planting at the bottom of slopes can help, as water will run down the slope to the plants – this is not an advantage if the area floods or gets waterlogged!

Once established, most plants should not require watering as they should develop a good root system. It is only some vegetables, fruits like strawberries, and bedding plants that may require regular watering, and this should only be necessary in real drought conditions. The timing of water application is important, as water applied during the middle of the day is likely to have up to 30 per cent evaporate, so is unavailable to the plant. The aim should be to apply water early morning, between 6am and 8am, or in the evening, between 6pm and 9pm – the temperature should be cool enough then for evaporation to be very low. In the summer, the evening is better as the temperature is cooling, the water will soak in and the roots can take it up overnight. In the morning, the temperatures are rising and some water could be evaporated (especially late morning).

The method of watering is also important, as the water should be directed to the base of the plant/root area where it should soak in and reach the roots. If applied generally to the border, the water that is not within reach of the roots will either evaporate or drain through the soil unless steps have been taken to hold that water, such as adding organic matter.

The frequency of watering is another factor to consider as this can affect the amount applied and how effective it is. It is far better to water heavily and infrequently, as small applications stay in the surface layer of the soil and therefore do not soak in enough to become available to the plant roots. This can result in a high loss of water by evaporation. It can also encourage plants to produce surface roots that quickly die in hot, dry weather, wasting the plants' energy and resources. Water should be provided at root level, or just above the roots, so that it soaks down into them. Annuals, vegetables and herbaceous perennials will make use of water at 10–15cm (4–6in) depth; shrubs, roses and trees will use 15cm (6in) and deeper water. Deep watering will encourage deep rooting, which makes the plant more resilient and drought tolerant.

Many gardeners water with watering cans or a hosepipe and assume they have applied sufficient water without checking. Once you have watered, take a trowel and dig a small hole in the area watered to check how deep the water has penetrated. Depending on the type and age of the plants being watered, the depth should be at least 10–15cm (4–6in) and, for established perennial plants, 20cm (8in). If watered to this depth, watering will only be required at ten to fourteen day intervals – longer if the soil is in good condition. Deep watering will encourage deeper root growth and make the plant more drought resistant in the future. If you are not sure whether watering is required, use a trowel to dig down to 10–15cm (4–6in) and check how dry the soil is. If the soil is moist at 7–10cm (3–4in) down, the plants will not need watering.

IRRIGATION

If droughts become hotter and more frequent, as in 2022, the requirement for irrigation will increase greatly, even though the supply of water will become more difficult. It is unlikely there will be sufficient water available to irrigate gardens as we have had in the past, and it will be necessary to make maximum use of any water available and to use it as efficiently as possible. There is an incentive for people on a water meter to not use too much water on their gardens as they are paying for what they use. Using less water on the garden reduces the strain on the reserves needed to supply people and the amount that must be treated for use via the mains. It is likely that water restriction will become more common, especially in the southeast of the country – another incentive to collect your own water! We need to design gardens to thrive – or at least survive – in the drought conditions of hot dry weather and lack of rain for long periods. Our choice of plants will have to change to suit the evolving conditions.

Established plants that are well cared for and in good soil should not require watering as they should have a good root system, capable of obtaining their water requirement. It should only be recently planted or young plants and plants for short-term use in the garden, like bedding plants, that need watering. Even in severe drought, most trees, shrubs and many herbaceous plants should be capable of getting the water they need in most soils, and water stress should only occur in exceptional droughts.

Add as much organic matter to the soil as possible, as mentioned in Chapter 2. Organic matter both holds water and improves the soil structure, which will help to reduce the amount of irrigation required. Good, well-structured and maintained soils will hold water better and may well require little – if any – watering, even during droughts.

At the initial design stage of a garden, try to design in a catchment area for rainfall and store or pump it into tanks for later use. Over the year in the UK, there is usually sufficient rainfall to supply most gardens and if it can be collected and stored for use when required, this would prevent most droughts from causing any problems. The aim of a good irrigation system is to direct the water to the root system and not on the leaves, where it will quickly evaporate.

Methods of Irrigation

Methods of water application vary from the very cheap, like the watering can, to the expensive, such as fully automatic irrigation systems. Watering cans are fine for watering greenhouses, small raised beds and containers, but can be heavy and time-consuming if a lot of watering is required. The main thing is to direct the water to the base of the plant or into the container, so none is wasted. Hosepipes can be inefficient at applying water unless the person holding them applies it directly to the soil above the root area. It is a waste of water to spray it over the plants and borders, as most of it will evaporate. Do not apply water under pressure as this will damage the soil structure and cause capping on some soils, which prevents rain from later entering the soil.

Moving up in sophistication are the various types of sprinklers, either rotary or oscillating. Rotary sprinklers, as the name suggests, spin around when applying water; oscillating sprinklers move from side to side. Using sprinklers on gardens is a wasteful use of water, which is going to become scarcer and more expensive in the future. Sprinklers apply large quantities of water to the area, but much can fall on the ground where there are no plant roots, including paths, patios or other hardstanding. When water falls on the soil it may not be absorbed by the plant roots but lost by evaporation. Also, sprinklers wet the foliage of the plants, which can encourage the spread of many fungal diseases. In the future we need to use irrigation systems that supply water directly to the soil adjacent to the plant so that it soaks down to the roots, and very little or no water is lost through evaporation.

Looking at more sustainable methods of irrigation, there are the drip, trickle and leaky or porous pipe systems. These are not too expensive, make efficient use of water and should be what gardeners look to use in the future. They are set up in the garden or to water containers, usually on a permanent or semi-permanent basis, and can be manually operated, semi-automatic or fully automatic on a timer. They can also be set up to water overnight when evaporation is lower as the temperature is cooler. The systems can be connected to the mains tap, but there must be a valve or break to prevent the back siphoning of water into the mains, which could cause food poisoning or other illnesses. If water butts or tanks have a pump or sufficient pressure, they can be connected to these systems.

Why Use Irrigation?

Before looking in more detail at the irrigation systems, we should consider what we are trying to achieve when irrigating plants. The aim is to get water down to the plants' roots for them to absorb it. Water only moves through the soil as it wets each layer; it does not drain straight down through the soil unless it is already damp or wet. As water percolates through the soil, it wets the soil particles and fills the small spaces between the particles (called pores). It moves down in millimetres at a time until it reaches the water table or parent rock, where it will stop and start to build up or flow sideways to springs, streams or ditches. The soil moisture deficit is the amount of water required to wet the soil to near field capacity, which is the maximum amount the soil will hold, measured in millimetres (it used to be in inches). Although it is not necessary to return the soil to field capacity, it is important to add a reasonable amount. So, when applying water to the soil, instead of thinking in litres you need to think in millimetres to ensure the water has soaked down to the plants' roots.

If the weather has been dry, sunny and warm, the water in the soil is used by the plants and some evaporates. The soil dries from the surface downwards, and to re-wet it the water is applied to the surface and moves down. If the soil is dry to a depth of 45mm (1¾in), to fully re-wet it we will need to apply approximately 45mm (1¾in) of water, which is equivalent to 4.5 litres (1 gallon) per 1m² (3¼ft²). If you consider a garden of 100m² (110yd²), to water the whole area would require 450 litres (99 gallons) of water. By using directed irrigation equipment, the water is placed directly over and around the root area and percolates down to the roots, using a lot less water while keeping the plants in a healthy condition.

Drip Irrigation

Drip irrigation (also called spaghetti system) is widely used commercially for watering plants in containers. Small pots will have one dripper per pot, while larger pots may have two to four drippers; very large containers use larger dripper nozzles and may have up to three. The system is supplied from a tank, mains or reservoir, along a main pipe. This divides down to a smaller pipe that runs along the rows of plants or containers, and from this pipe comes the dripper tube. When the irrigation is turned on, the water drips (hence the name) out of the tube into the container or around the plant. Owing to the size of the tube, the water is supplied very slowly so does not run off but soaks into the soil and down to the roots.

Drip irrigation is not too expensive, reasonably easy to set up and works on low water pressure, which can be handy in the garden. However, when working on the plants, the tubes can get in the way and be pulled out. If not replaced, the plant dies, not receiving the required amount of water. If you grow many plants in containers, such as pots, half-barrels, growbags, pouches on fences and so on, this system is very useful and works well. The containers can be changed and the dripper just inserted into the new container.

A drip irrigation system. Here it is used for watering trees in containers, but it can be used for any plants, containers or individual plants in the soil.

Trickle Irrigation

In trickle irrigation, again the main pipe comes from the source of water and divides down to a number of smaller pipes that run alongside the plants in a border or rows of vegetables. Where the pipe is close to a plant, a nozzle is inserted and the water trickles out of the nozzles and supplies the plants. Unplanted areas are not watered and the flow of water is controlled so none is wasted. The system is turned on for a set period sufficient to wet the soil down to the required level. Trickle systems are more widely used in commercial crop production than ornamental areas, but they can easily be adapted and, again, they are not too expensive.

An individual dripper.

Trickle hose watering alongside plants.

A trickle hose watering pear trees.

Leaky pipe irrigation system for pear trees.

A bedding scheme with a trickle hose set-up for watering.

Leaky or Porous Pipe Method

The final system is the leaky or porous pipe method. This is a pipe that is made to leak out water or allow water to pass through its structure and soak into the soil. They can be laid on the surface of the soil or under mulches, or shallowly buried in the soil as a permanent fixture. Again, the mains pipe supplies the water and smaller pipes connect to this – these are laid in the borders around the plants, working from one end of the border. The water leaks or drips out of the pipes, wets the soil underneath and soaks down to the plant roots.

Porous pipe can be purchased in rolls and fittings or in kits for certain sized borders. A typical kit would include 30m (33yd) of 16mm (½in) diameter pipe, 15m (16½yd) of hose (to connect to the tap), a tap connector,

Irrigation system set-up for watering newly planted asparagus beds at Wisley.

hose connector end bung and twenty barbed tees to hold the pipe in place. These are available in garden centres or via the internet.

Porous pipe is available in 5mm (¼in), 16mm (½in) and 20mm (¾in) diameters. The 5mm (¼in) is used in containers and sometimes sold as microbore tube. It uses 70 per cent less water than conventional watering and only needs 1.2 bar water pressure to supply 1–3 litres (¼–¾ gallons) per metre per hour. The 16mm (½in) is made from recycled materials and is the one commonly used for borders or watering vegetables and fruit. It works at 0.5–3 bar, delivers 2–6 litres (½–1¼ gallons) per metre per hour, and will work in up to 50m (55yd) lengths. The pipes should be spaced 30–60cm (12–24in) apart to water the whole area, but in borders place approximately 15–30cm (6–12in) from the plants. The 20mm (¾in) pipe is used commercially in landscaped borders and areas under mulching and has been used in sports fields and for vegetable and fruit growing. It works at 2–3 bar pressure, up to 80m (87yd) in length and applies 3–8 litres (¾–1¾ gallons) per metre per hour.

Layflat Tubing

Layflat tubing has been around for many years now and uses a thin polythene tube with perforations to deliver the water. It is rolled out where required and can be rolled back up at the end of the season, so is

reusable, with a lifespan of three to five years. After a while, the polythene becomes brittle and cracks. It is a cheap, easy-to-use system, which can be directly connected to the tap or hose.

Irrigation Tips

It is important that any water that is used in the above systems is clean, as small particles can easily block the nozzles or pipe. If water from ponds, lakes or uncovered tanks or recycled water is used, it is better to filter it to ensure it is clean and to avoid blockages.

Controls for a simple automatic watering system. This controls the watering of two raised beds growing vegetables. It waters twice a day, at 8am and 8pm.

Plastic layflat tubing – a cheap system, but the plastic is affected by UV light after a couple of years.

Liquid feed can be put through these systems when watering, but do not use any that may precipitate out in the pipes and, again, cause blockages. It is better to use a liquid concentrate rather than a powder.

All the above systems can be used by turning them on and off by hand or connecting them to some form of control system, which can make them semi- or fully automatic. The semi-automatic types often work by turning a knob, which starts the system and allows it to run for a set period. These are cheap and easy to use. Fully automatic types run off a battery or mains via a transformer, and can be programmed to come on and turn off at set times, as well as being capable of watering twice a day. Once programmed and set up, they will keep going until stopped or changed. These are very useful if you are away on holiday or for use at an allotment to save you having to visit every day. They also control the amount of water applied, so if set up correctly will not waste any.

OTHER WATERING METHODS

Moving on from irrigation systems, there are other methods of efficiently watering plants. If using outdoor taps for watering, ensure they are fitted with a non-return valve to prevent contaminated water flowing back into the drinking water.

Watering Young Trees and Shrubs

Young trees and shrubs may need watering until they are established – usually up to three years after planting. When planting a tree or shrub, install either a vertical pipe adjacent to the plant, a drainage pipe around the roots or a plastic soft drinks bottle at the side of each plant – these will supply water directly to the roots. Doing any of these is relatively simple.

Vertical Pipe

To install a vertical pipe, dig the hole for the tree slightly larger and set a 60cm (24in) to 1m (3¼ft) length of pipe vertically adjacent to the tree. The length of the pipe will vary, depending on the depth of the planting hole: a 5–10cm (2–4in) diameter pipe is sufficient. Backfill the hole and firm as usual to plant the tree. The first watering

Two perforated drainage pipes used for watering trees; the pipes go down to under the trees' root systems so they receive water where required. Water is applied via the pipes.

can be over the surface area and allowed to soak down to the roots. Subsequent waterings are down the pipe, which directs the water straight to the roots and soaks the surrounding soil, with no evaporation.

Drainage Pipe

The drainage pipe method is similar: dig out the hole, put the tree in position and wrap the drainage pipe around and over the roots. Backfill as usual, ensuring there are no air pockets left by firming and watering. The bottom end of the pipe has a bung fitted to stop the water flowing straight out and the top can have a cap fitted to stop debris getting in and blocking it. The water is again put down the pipe. It comes out of the holes in the drainage pipe directly to the roots and soaks the surrounding soil.

Plastic Drinks Bottles

Possibly more suitable for the gardener is to insert a plastic soft drinks bottle next to each tree and shrub. Remove the base of the bottle first, then bury it in the soil so it just sticks out above the soil with what was the top now in the soil. Water is poured into the open base area and soaks around the roots. Smaller drinks bottles can be used for herbaceous plants. A similar idea to sinking a plastic soft drinks bottle into the soil is to do the same with a plastic flowerpot and water the plant via this – again, it directs water down to the roots.

Proprietary Tree-watering Devices

There are also proprietary tree-watering devices available. One is called the Tree Gator and is placed around the tree and filled with water when required. The water soaks into the soil slowly, watering the tree.

Tree Gator – a proprietary tree watering system. Water is applied via the bag and gradually soaks into the soil, over the roots.

A second type of Tree Gator system for tree watering.

An irrigated tree in a drought-affected lawn.

Using Water-retaining Granules

A different approach is to look at holding water in the soil or container. This can be achieved by using water-retaining granules, usually made from synthetic polyacrylamide or polymers. They are brought as dry crystals, looking like large sugar granules, and are mixed with the growing media or soil at a set rate (*see* the packet instructions).

When watering the soil, the crystals absorb the water and hold it, but it is still available to the plants. When the crystals have absorbed water, they swell up and turn into a jelly, which also holds nutrients. They are useful in containers and small areas of soil, like raised beds, but are too expensive for large areas of the garden or allotment. They were originally used in hanging baskets and worked well; they can now be purchased as small mats that are used to line the basket and can hold enough water to last up to a fortnight.

RAINWATER COLLECTION

In domestic premises, the main area of collection is from the roofs of houses, garages, conservatories, porches, sheds and greenhouses. Water is collected via the downpipe, either straight into the water butt or tank or through a diverter from the downpipe to the water butt. Any building with guttering can be used to collect water. Aim to collect the maximum amount possible – it is highly unlikely you will have too much, so it will not go to waste. During some of the heavy storms in 2022, my 200-litre (44-gallon) water butts filled up within a couple of hours from water collected from the house roof!

The weather is becoming more unpredictable, so we need to be prepared to collect rain whenever it occurs and have collection and storage facilities set up for it. It is possible to collect 40–50,000 litres of water per year from the average house in the UK. This is more than enough to water most gardens; it is just a case of finding space to store it. All new houses should be fitted with large underground tanks under the drive, parking area or lawn, to store the rainwater for use both in the garden and for flushing toilets.

Rainwater is the best water to use for watering as it does not contain any chemicals like fluoride, has a slightly acidic pH and is suitable for all plants, even orchids and ericaceous plants. If stored correctly it should not contain any plant diseases and will keep for years, if necessary (unlikely in today's climate!).

Water Storage

Rainwater can be collected in water butts, tanks (both above and below ground), recycled containers, barrels, drums, ponds, lakes, ditches, natural swimming ponds, water bowsers... in fact any container that will hold water! The larger these are, the better, as the more water they will hold, but they will need to be in relation to the size of your garden.

One disadvantage of adapting containers for storing water is they can suddenly leak for no apparent reason, other than the fact there is a weakness somewhere in the container. I have had this happen on a few occasions and put it down to the weight of water pressure forcing a minute crack in the container. The size of container can vary from 20 litres (4½ gallons) up to 3,000 litres (660 gallons) or more – it will depend on the space available. The larger the container and the more you have, the more water can be stored available for watering.

Four water butts linked together, giving a greater volume of water collection.

Water butt collecting water from the roof of a polytunnel.

Water can be collected from the roofs of houses, conservatories, greenhouses, polytunnels, sheds or any other building you have access to that has guttering and a downpipe to connect. It is just a case of connecting a diverter to the downpipe and diverting the water into the water butt. To increase storage capacity, a line of water butts can be connected and linked to one downpipe.

The average-sized house in the UK can collect over 40,000 litres (8,800 gallons) of water; this varies depending on what part of the country you live, as the western side of the UK is wetter than the eastern side. It is easy to calculate how much water it is possible to collect by multiplying the surface area of the roof by the rainfall in millimetres per year. Calculate 80 per cent, as this allows for loss by evaporation and overflowing of the gutters in heavy storms. It is surprising how much can be collected from small greenhouse roofs.

Once the water butts are full, allow any surplus to run onto the beds, borders or lawn to top the soil up to field capacity (the maximum amount of water the soil will hold after any drainage water has left it). Also fill up any watering cans, buckets or other small containers that will hold water and can be used for watering.

If you are having any construction work carried out on the house or garden, if possible have an underground water tank installed under the drive, patio or similar area. These will hold 3,000 litres (660 gallons) of water or more. They just require a small pump installed to pump the water to the irrigation system, or even to flush the toilet, which will help to reduce the water bill if on a meter.

As water is becoming scarcer and more expensive, in the future it will be wise to try to use recycled water or rainwater for our irrigation. A large amount of rain falls in the winter when it is not required on the garden, so this needs storing until the spring and summer. Rainwater is well worth storing as it is free, clean, has a slightly acidic pH that is suitable for most plants and is able to be stored for long periods.

Tanks and water butts should, where possible, be covered to prevent dirt, leaves and mosquitos getting in. If possible, they should be on a stand with a tap fitted, which makes getting the water out easier than dunking in a watering can. If the tanks are large enough or the water butt is on a stand or on higher ground, a hose can be fitted and the water directed straight to the plants. Underground tanks will need to be fitted with a pump to push the water up to ground level, and all tanks or large storage facilities could also be fitted with a pump to make watering easier and allow the use of automatic irrigation systems.

USING RECYCLED (GREY) WATER

Recycled (grey) water is water that has been used in the house for washing, showering and bathing, or from the washing machine or kitchen sink, as long as it has not been contaminated with grease or chemicals. According to figures from the water industry, the average household uses approximately 350 litres (77 gallons) of water a day. Some of this will be flushed down the toilet and some drunk, but at least 200 litres (44 gallons) is likely to be available as grey water that could be used on the garden.

Using grey water makes very good use of a waste resource and saves it having to be treated at the sewerage works and pumped into a river, which can cause problems further downstream, for example causing large blooms of algae in some areas of water. Using grey water also saves using expensively treated tap water in the garden; the water is effectively used twice: once for washing or similar and again in the garden to help the plants grow. This saves a valuable resource in water that may become more valuable as climate change evolves.

If you have a septic tank system, using grey water will also save you money – less water is sent to the tank so it will need emptying less often. If on a water meter, it prevents having to pay for letting water go down the drains! Using grey water conserves water, which is important in drought conditions that are likely to occur more often in the future. It also saves energy and the cost of treating the water in the first place.

How to Use Grey Water

Grey water is ideal for watering trees, shrubs, hedges, fruit trees and perennial flowering plants, but avoid using it on vegetables, which could be contaminated. Do not use grey water too often on ericaceous plants or on the same area as it may raise the soil pH slightly. It is fine to use on top and bush fruit (but not strawberries, as these could be contaminated) and is useful on herbaceous plants, bedding plants, trees and shrubs, as well as container-grown plants. If you still have some surplus grey water, use it on the lawn to keep it green. Any waste uncontaminated water can be used to keep the soil moist during droughts and other dry periods.

Ensure the water is not polluted with anything that may affect the plants or soil – most soaps, shampoos and washing-up liquids are not a problem. Water from dishwashers can have a high salt content so may be better not used on the garden, or you can dilute it with additional water. If using water from washing machines, check the washing powder is low in phosphorous and sodium, as these can affect the soil structure of clay soils and possible plant growth. One method of reducing the amount of water flushed down the toilet is to collect the urine and use it as an activator on your compost heap or to feed plants. There is a reasonable amount of nitrogen and potash in urine, which can be used to feed herbaceous plants and shrubs.

I have used grey water on my garden and on plants in containers for over twenty years now and not had any problems. I often water my plants in containers using water I have washed the vegetables in or used for hand washing in the kitchen, so it does not contain any contaminants other than a little soap.

Grey water should be used soon after its original use. If stored, it tends to start to smell and it could become infected with bacteria, although there are some treatments that can be used to allow the water to be stored for a short period. It can be piped straight from the bathroom (if upstairs) by gravity onto garden borders using pipes or guttering. These just need adjusting or moving so the same area is not watered continuously. It is possible to have a permanent irrigation system set up to use the grey water from the house. Although this is more appropriate for drier climates, we may need to consider this in the future as the climate in the UK becomes drier, especially on free-draining sandy soils.

Grey water is produced every day (unless away on holiday), all the year round, so is a reliable source of water – and at no cost as it has already been used. It can be applied to the garden using watering cans or buckets (or any other available container) or can be pumped via a hosepipe onto the garden. Simple systems, as mentioned above, will work by gravity if the house if higher than the garden. Washing machines have their own pump so will start the water flowing in the right direction and, if downhill, will flow a good distance. If you decide to install a pump and more complex system, it can pay to filter the water to avoid it blocking nozzles and small-diameter pipes. The grey water can be fed into a tank for short-term storage and then pumped to where required, and it can be pumped uphill if necessary. If filtered, the filters will need cleaning at regular intervals.

Using Grey Water Safely

Grey water is quite safe to use on ornamental plants, top fruit and bush fruit (but keep it off the fruit itself) but it is not recommended for use on vegetables, especially salad leaves and similar crops. It is not safe to drink or ingest and can harm some aquatic wildlife if it gets into ponds. Do not apply by sprinkler systems, as it could be accidentally ingested or fine droplets breathed in if nearby. Also avoid puddles or standing water as these smell and children could play in them. Do not use greasy water or water that contains cooked food scraps, as this can attract vermin.

CONTAINER GROWING

One disadvantage of container growing is that containers need a lot of watering over the summer period, especially if the weather is dry. This is both

Self-watering containers – water is supplied by a reservoir that is topped up by the tanks at the rear. This system just needs the tanks to be filled up once a week.

time-consuming and needs a decent supply of water, or is expensive in tap water if on a water meter. With the likelihood of summer droughts and wet periods in the winter increasing in the future, we will need to modify the methods we use for container growing.

Try to use the largest containers possible as they hold the most growing media (also called compost) and therefore usually the largest amount of water. Also add water-absorbing granules to hold more water and choose growing media that will hold water rather than being free draining, unless growing cacti, succulents or alpines that prefer good drainage. If using terracotta containers, line the inside with an old polythene bag to reduce water loss through the clay container. During the summer, place containers in trays, saucers, lids or similar containers to catch any drainage water from watering and rain; this saves it going to waste and makes it available for the plants to use. Water either early morning or late evening in the summer, as there is less evaporation then. In the winter, place the containers on feet to improve the drainage, especially during wet periods or heavy rain; waterlogged planters soon result in plant death, owing to lack of oxygen.

Self-watering containers and hanging baskets are a big advantage as they have a reservoir in the base that holds water and they slowly release this to the growing media and plants as required via a wick. They are more expensive, but can save a lot of water and your plants!

Hydroponics

Having a section on hydroponics in a book on adapting to climate change may seem a bit odd, but most hydroponic systems recycle water so have a low over-all water consumption, even in hot weather. Very little water is lost by evaporation and it is recycled in the system until the plants use it.

Hydroponics is when water is used as the main growing media, or in conjunction with an inert media such as rockwool, clay pellets, perlite, or occasionally coir or a similar media. It can be used to grow vegetables, some fruits and flowers, and vertical gardens, but is not used as part of the general garden design. It is a production method for food, in particularly tomatoes, peppers, cucumbers and melons, and some lettuces are also grown using it. The nutrient film technique (NFT) is the main commercial method of growing the crops mentioned above and is widely used in greenhouse production in the UK and Holland.

Hydroponics is an enclosed system so there is no runoff, evaporation or wastewater. Water can be recycled until taken up by plants, as also are the nutrients in the water. The main disadvantage of hydroponics is the initial cost of the equipment and setup. Once purchased and set up, there are few running costs other than electricity for the pump (if it is a circulating system) and the fertiliser for feed. If keen, you could move a stage further to aquaponics, where fish are raised along with the plants and you get two crops from the same area and resource. The fish waste feeds the plants and the plants' roots help to clean the water – a very sustainable system.

Hydroponics has several advantages. It can produce larger plants more quickly and give higher yields than conventional growing methods, especially indoors, but the systems will need good maintenance and care to ensure there are no problems. No growing media is required for most systems; water usage is low and there is less disease, as long as good hygiene is followed. The systems can be homemade or brought as a kit of any size. Do some research and see which system will suit you, the plants you grow and your growing methods.

Here I will briefly look at some of the systems that can be used by gardeners, both indoors and outdoors. They are very useful if there is no soil available, such as in a concrete yard area. Most vertical growing systems use hydroponics and these will be used to produce more food in the future, especially in urban areas and as land becomes more expensive. There are many systems of hydroponics, but we will focus on just six of them: drip, NFT, deep water culture, ebb and flow, wick and aeroponics.

Drip System

This is similar to the drip irrigation system mentioned above, consisting of small narrow tubes connected to a feeder pipe that is fed from the reservoir. It drips the water and nutrients onto the substrate in which the plant is growing; the substrate can be coir, rockwool or a mix of inert materials. The water is pumped from the reservoir to drippers where it drips onto the substrate and drains back to the reservoir via a tray or trough. The pump can be set to come on by a timer so can be automatic. It is an easy system that is not too expensive and can be used for lettuce, strawberries, onions, cucumbers and other crops.

Nutrient Film Technique

As stated earlier, this is widely used commercially with many hundreds of hectares of greenhouses using this system. Most of the tomatoes, cucumbers and peppers sold in the UK are grown using NFT. The plants are grown in a covered trough set at a slight slope. Water is pumped from the reservoir to the top of the trough and flows down by gravity back to the reservoir. As it trickles down the trough, it baths the roots in water and they absorb some of the water and nutrients. It is possible to achieve very high yields using NFT and it is fairly easy to operate, with the pump being the only working part.

Lettuce in NFT channels, fed by the narrow pipes on the left. A futuristic method used in vertical growing of lettuce on shelves.

Herbs growing in plastic NFT channels. The water flows from right to left and returns to the tank via the gutter.

Salad leaves, growing in NFT channels on shelving.

Deep Water Culture

There are a number of deep water cultures available, many sold under various trade names. The plants are suspended above the reservoir and the roots grow down into the water and just above it. The water is oxygenated by a small air pump to provide oxygen for the roots. It is an easy system to set up, simple to use and a good starter for beginners. It has been used for growing lettuce, basil, kale, chard and similar vegetables.

Ebb and Flow

This is widely used by pot plant growers in greenhouses to produce begonias, pot chrysanthemums and roses. Plants are grown in troughs, in trays or on benches. Water is pumped from the reservoir to these, where it flows down into a gutter and returns to the reservoir. This is repeated a number of times each day, depending on the weather and water requirement for the plants.

The trays, troughs or benches are flooded for a short time while the water flows down and then they are dry, hence the name ebb and flow (sometimes called flood system). The roots can take up oxygen while the plant is in the dry phase. This is not an expensive system, is easy to set up and can be used to grow many types of plants.

Wick

A simple, easy and cheap system and a good starting point to try hydroponics. Again, there is a reservoir – this time usually under the plant container – and they are connected by a wick, hence the name. The wick is made from capillary matting or a similar material that allows water to flow up it. The plant takes up water from the substrate or growing media and that water is replaced by the wick from the reservoir. It is just a case of keeping the reservoir topped up, especially during hot periods. Wicks work well for small plants like lettuce, chard, spinach, small herbs and many flowering plants.

Aeroponics

An expensive system but one that will give high yields. The plants are suspended above a container, with their roots hanging down. A pump sprays the roots with water, containing the feed, at regular intervals, as the roots are not in the water but above it in the atmosphere – they therefore have a ready supply of oxygen they can absorb. The plants do not make a large amount of root growth as they are readily supplied with water and nutrients, so do not require many roots. The main disadvantage is the initial cost and checking the pumps, as if these fail the plants die very quickly. Aeroponics can be used for any plants.

CHAPTER 5

GREEN ROOFS, LIVING WALLS AND RAIN GARDENS

To help overcome the effects of climate change, we need to make maximum use of all available areas, including, where possible, roofs and walls. Roofs can be used to produce renewable energy or heat water, but an alternative is to create a roof garden. This can be done on both flat and sloping roofs and can be an area for plants or a complete landscaped garden. Flat roofs can also be used for relaxation and entertaining.

These adaptations can be expensive and can involve a lot of work. If a house roof is to be converted or built as a green roof, you will certainly need good advice on its construction and maintenance. Even small roofs like sheds, porches or garages need strong supports to hold the weight of a green roof, but this will be more feasible than converting a house roof.

GREEN ROOFS

Green roofs have been constructed on houses, bungalows, offices, warehouses, schools, factories, housing developments, sheds, garages, house extensions and many other buildings. The garden can range from a covering of low-growing plants over the whole roof to a fully landscaped garden with borders, shrubs, trees, patios and barbecues. Most green roofs are created for visual appearances and to create a biodiverse habitat rather than to be used as a garden to visit, relax in or grow fruit and vegetables in, although some are, especially on apartment blocks.

A wide range of plants can be grown including grasses, wildflowers, groundcover plants, herbaceous plants, small shrubs, climbers and trees. Although most green roofs are planted with low-growing evergreens, often succulent plants thrive in such conditions without requiring too much maintenance.

Green roofs have several advantages including reducing the amount and speed of water flowing from the roof, which is useful for storm water management and contributes greatly to reducing flooding. Some of the water will be used by the plants on the roof so less goes down into the drainage system, reducing the chance of it being overwhelmed and sewage getting into the rivers and coastal waters. The plants on the roof absorb carbon dioxide – not a large amount but some – and this all helps to reduce the effects of climate change; the more green roofs and living walls we have, the better.

Roof gardens also help to insulate the roof, both in summer and winter. During hot weather, they keep buildings cooler, reducing the need for air conditioning and therefore energy use. In the winter, they reduce the heat loss and need for as much energy to heat buildings. They are also very useful in reducing wind chill, which can be a major factor in lowering the building temperature.

Plants are very good at reducing the amount of dust and air pollution, producing a healthier environment, especially for people with asthma and other respiratory diseases. Leaves also collect gases and heavy metal dust from traffic and industry, which is why trees are so useful in cities to clean the air. Both green roofs and living walls reduce noise; living walls have been constructed alongside busy roads to help reduce the noise and pollution.

Roof areas are vastly underutilised; they basically just provide a cover for the building but could also provide a habitat for many creatures, especially birds and insects. As well as absorbing carbon dioxide, they produce oxygen, and, if visible, they look far more attractive than flat or tiled roofs. Any food grown on roofs will be fresh and local, so will reduce food miles, and this will also increase the amount of food produced in the UK without using more land.

Before building or converting to a green roof, it is critical to ensure the roof framework is strong enough to hold the additional weight, not just of the plants and substrate but also of the water during rainstorms. A shallow green roof of 5–7cm (2–3in) depth may not be too heavy but will be well above what most roof structures were designed to hold; a 10–15cm (4–6in) deep green roof will be very heavy. Roof structures can be strengthened, but this is expensive and is not always feasible; however, it is not too difficult with sheds and small garden buildings. Where new buildings are being constructed, the roof can be designed to hold the weight of a roof garden and this may not greatly increase the cost. If your roof is not strong enough, consider living walls or vertical gardens.

A small roof garden on a shed is not too difficult to make and many DIYers could do this, including strengthening the roof by fixing extra supports and braces or roof trusses. The growing media and waterproofing layer need to be suitable, as do the plants used; they need to be adapted to the conditions on the roof, which can be exposed, very hot, windy or cold. Being exposed means the plants suffer the full effects of winds, gales, sun, frost, snow and hail, as well as bright light on hot sunny days, which can dry the roof and plants quickly.

Green Roof Construction

Green roofs are made up of several layers. These will vary depending on the type and sophistication of the green roof and planting. Green roofs on houses, apartments and offices are often large areas and may have a range of herbaceous plants that need a depth of substrate. This will be heavy, whereas green roofs on sheds, bike stores, bin stores or similar buildings may only need a thin layer of substrate over a waterproof and drainage layer.

It is important to be aware of the additional weight of the roof garden so that the roof can be strengthened. Even a lightweight system can increase the weight of the roof by 70–170kg (11–27 stone) per 1m^2 (3¼ft^2) and if soil-based substrate is to be used by

A green roof on a shelter with sedum growing on it.

Mixed green roof on a bug hotel. The plants are too widely spaced, so take time to cover the area.

290–970kg (46–153 stone) per 1m² (3¼ft²) (Dunnett and Kingsbury). Snow and water can also cause additional weight. These are considerable weights, so an expert will need to be consulted before starting.

Factors to Consider

On a small building like a shed, porch or store, the roof can be supported by a framework constructed on the outside of the building, just to hold the weight of the green roof, so that no additional weight is put onto the building itself. If the green roof is not too heavy, extra beams, trusses, braces and supports can be fitted to both the building and roof. Using very shallow depths of a lightweight substrate with small plants like sedum can keep the weight down. If using a wider range of plants that need a deeper substrate of 10–15cm (4–6in), this will be much heavier – in fact, at least twice the weight – and the roof will need to be designed accordingly.

Another factor to consider is whether it is a sloping or flat roof. If the roof is sloping, there is a limit to how steep the slope can be to be able to still hold the roof garden, or it could slide off. Slopes greater than 15 to 17 per cent will be unstable; even with shallower slopes it would be wise to have cross battens or a box construction to hold the substrate and plants in place. All green roofs will have a waterproof layer, which is likely to be smooth, leading to the material above it sliding down. If a box system is used, a roof of up to 55 per cent can be constructed. The box system can be made of wood, which is fairly heavy, or plastic grids are available.

The wooden edging to the green roof.

Plastic modular system for a green roof to hold the growing media in place.

Ensure the edge of the roof garden is well secured, especially if it is holding any of the weight. This also stops the wind getting under the material and lifting any off. A wood strip, stones, small paving slabs or concrete edging kerbs can be used to keep everything in position.

With the right choice of plants, irrigation should not be needed; if the building is low, aiming a hose over the roof should be sufficient. If decorative plants or vegetables are to be grown, some type of irrigation system will be required. Where possible, recycle rainwater collected previously from the roof via the downpipe and stored in a tank or water butt, and then pump back up onto the roof.

Starting Construction

Once sure about the weight-bearing capacity of the roof, construction can start. If an existing roof is to be used, clean off any dirt and loose material and then lay the waterproofing or weatherproofing layer to prevent any water gaining access to the roof. The waterproofing layer needs to be long-lasting, so do not choose a cheap material that can deteriorate quickly. Thick PVC or a butyl pond liner are suitable for most roofs, such as on sheds and garages. If possible, use one sheet to cover the whole roof or ensure any joints are well-sealed and overlapped; keep this sheet covered so it is not damaged by the sun's ultraviolet light.

Over the waterproof layer add a root protection barrier to prevent any roots getting through to the waterproof layer and damaging it – or, even worse, getting to the roof structure. This layer can be a thick (1mm or thicker) sheet of PVC, well-sealed if it has any joints. If there are any higher walls at the edge of the roof, fold the sheet up so that roots cannot get below it.

The next layer is the drainage layer, which prevents any build-up of water on the roof or ponding and stops the substrate becoming too wet and causing water-logging and plant rot, especially as many of the plants are chosen to grow in dry conditions. Drainage matting like capillary matting is available. Lay this over the root protection layer and hold it in place with a 5–8cm (2–3in) depth of gravel, stone chippings or expanded clay granules – gravel and stone are heavy, so this should be kept in mind. On sloping roofs, a drainage layer may not be required as the water will flow down via gravity and out into the gutter.

Above the drainage layer a filter matting should be added, which prevents the substrate being washed into the drainage layer, possibly causing blockages. The final layer is the substrate of growing media, which should be as lightweight as possible and have good drainage, but still retain some water for the plants. Soil tends to be too heavy, hold too much water and the fine clays get washed into the filter layer or cap on the surface. Unless very sandy, they tend to slump, which reduces the drainage capacity even more. Avoid using too much organic matter as this will decompose over time, then the growing media shrinks and tends to compact.

It is best to use a manmade mix for the growing media, which is free draining and lightweight but holds a small amount of water and nutrients. The following materials have been used in mixtures: sand, pumice, small gravel, lightweight expanded clay aggregate (LECA), crushed bricks or concrete. LECA is light in weight, holds some water and can be used on its own or in mixtures; it has been widely used in indoor plant displays, so is well tried and tested. A mixture of LECA and crushed bricks gives an open mix; not too heavy nor expensive and holds some water.

The depth of the substrate depends on the range of plants to be grown, sedums and sempervivums only need 3–5cm (2–3in), but for grasses and other small herbaceous plants, 10–15cm (4–6in) is required, however this is much heavier. Modular or plastic grid

systems are available, which are fitted over the root protection layer; these hold the growing media and plants and are reasonably easy to change, if required. The modules come in various depths, depending on the range of plants grown – very shallow for sedums and deeper for herbaceous plants.

Green Roof Maintenance

Green roofs do not require a great deal of maintenance, which, owing to their location, is a good thing. The following four tasks are all that is required most years:

Weeding

As the substrate should not contain any weed seeds or perennial weed roots, there should not be any weeds growing during the first couple of years. After that, it will only be weeds that have seed dispersed by wind which are blown onto the substrate or seeds deposited by birds. These should be removed before they become established, especially if tree seedlings or perennial weeds. An annual or twice-yearly hand weed should be sufficient to keep the roof garden tidy and weed-free.

Drainage

Check the gutters and downpipes to ensure they do not become blocked as this can cause the gutters to overflow or the water to back up into the drainage layer on the roof, adding additional weight and possibly killing some of the plants that are not adapted to wet conditions. Check the drainage layer has not become silted up with fine particles or organic matter – this should not happen, but if it does it will need flushing out.

Trimming

If very dwarf plants like sedums and sempervivums are chosen, no trimming will be required. Larger herbaceous plants will need an annual trim back in late autumn or winter. Any annual plants will need removing after flowering and the seeds have dropped onto the substrate.

Feeding

Once the green roof is established, an annual feed with a slow-release fertiliser will keep it growing without it becoming too rampant. It should only be a light feed at the lower rate recommended by the fertiliser manufacturers. As the substrate is free draining it will not hold any nutrients, so an annual feed will keep the plants healthy and less prone to stress.

If you have a small roof over a bin store or cycle rack, it will be well worth trying a green roof to improve the appearance and provide an extra growing area.

Sedums for Green Roofs

There are a number of plants suitable for green roofs (*see* Plants for Green Roofs), but the sedums and plants listed below are tried and tested, have been widely used and are very reliable.

- *Sedum acre* – has bright yellow flowers, which are liked by bees, and is commonly available and easy to grow. It is considered by some to be a bit of a weed.
- *Sedum album* – produces white flowers in June. The leaves go purple-brown during drought conditions but soon recover once the rains arrive.
- *Sedum kamtschaticum floriferum* 'Weihenstephaner Gold' – has yellow flowers during the summer with green foliage that goes bronze in the winter.
- *Sedum rupestre* – a more vertical sedum than the above. Has a flower spike up to 30cm (12in) tall with yellow flowers.
- *Sedum sexangulare* – has tiny yellow flowers in the summer, grows up to 10cm (4in) and spreads fairly quickly.
- *Sedum spathulifolium* – widely used by parks departments in carpet beds. It is very tough and reliable and has silver-grey leaves tinted with purple and yellow flowers.
- *Sedum spathulifolium* 'Purpureum' – a purple-leaved form of the above, again with yellow flowers, and very reliable.
- *Sedum spathulifolium* 'Cape Blanco' – a grey-leaved cultivar, again widely used in carpet bedding and floral clocks. Produces clusters of yellow flowers in the summer.
- *Sedum spurium* – has pink or white flowers in late summer. It grows to a height of 10cm (4in) and is reasonably vigorous.

Sempervivums for Green Roofs

Sempervivums are another succulent that go well with sedums. They form clumps or rosettes that give a contrast to the sedum habit of growth. They are very good in drought conditions and have grown on roofs for centuries, hence their common name 'houseleeks'.

- *Sempervivum arachnoideum* – commonly called the 'cobweb' sempervivum as the leaves appear to be covered in cobwebs, which are actually a dense covering of hairs.
- *Sempervivum tectorum* – the common houseleek with a mat-forming habit of growth, made up of a number of closely growing rosettes. Has purple flowers and the foliage has reddish-purple tips to greyish-green succulent leaves.

Also worth considering if some flower colour is preferred is *Delosperma cooperi*. This drought-tolerant plant has pink, purple, red or white flowers in the summer. It is hardy in the south of the UK, with a height of 10cm (4in).

Sedum spathulifolium 'Purpurem' – a useful sedum for green roofs as it is low-growing, has attractive foliage, produces yellow flowers in the summer and survives drought well.

Plants for Green Roofs

The following plants have all been successfully used on green roofs, even in substrate of less than 7cm (3in):

- *Achillea millefolium*
- *Allium schoenoprasum*
- *Armeria maritima*
- *Briza media*
- *Delosperma cooperi*
- *Euphorbia cyparissias*
- *Leontodon autumnalis*
- *Lotus corniculatus*
- *Saponaria ocymoides*
- *Sedum* and *sempervivum* species (*see* separate lists)
- *Teucrium chamaedrys*
- *Thymus serpyllum*

The following plants need a substrate depth of 10cm (4in) or more (15cm/6in will be sufficient):

- *Acaena microphylla*
- *Achillea millefolium*
- *Antennaria dioica*
- *Armeria juniperifolia*
- *Armeria maritima*
- *Campanula carpatica*
- *Cerastium tomentosum*
- *Chiastophyllum oppositifolium*
- *Dryas octopetala*
- *Festuca glauca*
- *Phlox subulata*
- *Pulsatilla vulgaris*
- *Raoulia australis*

Bulbs for Roof Gardens

Providing there is sufficient depth of substrate, the following bulbs will grow in roof gardens:

- *Anemone blanda*
- *Allium christophii*
- *Allium schoenoprasum*
- *Allium moly*
- *Crocus chrysanthus*
- *Crocus tommasinianus*
- *Nerine bowdenii*
- *Scilla biflora*
- *Scilla mischtschenkoana*
- *Scilla siberica*

Sempervivum 'Red Beauty' – useful on roof gardens and vertical walls.

LIVING WALLS, VERTICAL GARDENING OR FAÇADE GREENING

The use of climbing plants or wall shrubs growing up building walls has been around for centuries and is useful in covering ugly walls and fences. Vertical gardening has been around for a few decades now, but is not as widely used or known about. Walls can be used to grow foliage, flowering plants, or vegetables, herbs and fruit, and growing plants on walls makes very good use of a surface area that is otherwise wasted. There are many sites where climbing or wall-trained plants could be used, including houses, office blocks, factories, community buildings and multi-storey car parks, as well as boundary and other walls or fences.

In this section, I will look at the two main methods of using walls to grow plants: the first using climbing and wall shrubs, which is the conventional method; the second using modular systems to grow plants on the wall, which are mainly based on hydroponic systems. Both make very good use of space, improve the appearance of many buildings, absorb carbon dioxide and produce oxygen, as well as cleaning some of the pollution from the air. They also insulate the building, in both summer and winter, and can reduce noise all the year round.

Climbers give summer cooling as they reduce the amount of heat absorbed by the walls, and the leaves transpire water, which has a cooling and humidifying effect. During the winter, evergreen climbers provide insulation by reducing the effects of wind, especially cold winds that have a wind-chill effect and high winds that draw the heat out of buildings. The plants also trap air between the plant and wall – this, as well as the density of plant growth, acts as an insulator.

Both evergreen and deciduous plants screen large walls and reduce the stark look of buildings, especially

Apples and pears trained in an S-shape, making very good use of the wall space and giving interest to the area.

Ficus carica (fig), growing on a wall, making use of the wall space to produce fruit and a decorative effect.

newly constructed ones. There are climbers available that can climb up four or more storeys, giving a large surface area for leaves to absorb carbon dioxide, reducing pollution and noise, and insulating the building. The surface area of the leaves will be the equivalent of a medium-sized tree, without taking up any space.

Green walls provide habitats for many insects and birds, including nesting sites, and flowering plants are a source of nectar and pollen. Grapes, blackberries and similar plants will give a good crop of fruit, helping to make the household more self-sufficient. Fruit trees can be trained against walls, making the area productive as well as decorative. They can be trained as espaliers, fans and cordons, and also various shapes such as circles, W- or S-shapes.

Climbers

There are three main methods of supporting plants on buildings, walls and fences. Firstly use self-clinging plants like ivy, which have small roots that cling to the wall. Secondly, fix wires to the wall either vertically or horizontally to suit the plant being grown. Thirdly, use trellis or mesh, which again is fixed to the wall – these are used to support plants that twine around them or plants that are trained along wires.

Wire supports may look a bit utilitarian, but wooden trellises painted with one of the coloured preservatives can be an attractive feature on their own and can be used for any climbing plant. Other supporting materials include galvanised or plastic-coated weldmesh,

Apple tree trained in a circle to add interest as well as produce fruit.

Clematis montana 'Alba' will cover a large area and gives a colourful late spring flower display.

Hedera helix 'Buttercup' – provides yellow foliage for most of the year and is self-supporting.

building reinforcing which has the Corten steel effect. Stainless steel or other bright steel wire well-fixed to the wall can form a feature and once the plants are established, little of it can be seen.

Choosing Plants

When choosing which plants to grow, consider the following points:

- Evergreen or deciduous – a mix of both can look a bit patchy if not used carefully.
- Height of the plant and the area to be covered – too vigorous a plant may need constant pruning back; a less-vigorous plant may not cover the required area.
- Type of support required – is the plant self-clinging, a twiner or trained on wires or other supports?
- Aspect of the wall:
  - South-facing walls allow the growing of more tender plants, especially with increasing temperatures and milder winters. They are very useful for fruits such as apricots, nectarines and peaches.
  - North-facing walls have a more limited range of plants but there are still plenty available, including wall-trained gooseberries, climbing hydrangea or variegated ivies. North-facing walls have lower light and sun levels and are cooler than the other aspects.

Campsis radicans – a summer-flowering climber that will cover a large area of wall and has bright orange flowers in the summer through to the autumn.

o East-facing walls receive good light, but in the spring some plants are prone to frost damage as the plants warm up too quickly from the early morning sun.

o West-facing walls are usually warm as they get the afternoon and evening sun and are often suitable for a similar range of plants to south-facing walls.

● Microclimate and the direction of the prevailing wind (usually from the southwest in most parts of the UK) – this can affect the temperature against a wall. Is there shade from adjacent buildings or trees or frost pockets (especially if cold air drains down to the wall)? A wind-tunnel effect along the wall can both damage the plant and increases transpiration, stressing the plant if it is not adapted to these conditions.

Planting

Climbers and wall shrubs should be planted in a good, fertile soil that will hold moisture, as soil is often dry adjacent to walls. This will usually entail improving the soil, as against walls it can be poor quality and may contain builders' rubbish, which should be removed (unless planting a fig tree, which is better in a restricted root run). Mix in 30 to 40 per cent of organic matter and some slow-release fertiliser to get the plants established. Mycorrhiza is well worth using to get the plants established – the roots can be dipped into a paste, or the powder sprinkled into the planting hole. Plant at the same depth as it is in the pot, firm in and water, then cover a 1m (3¼ft) radius with mulch to a depth of 5–10cm (2–4in).

Maintenance

Watering

As it is usually very dry against a wall, the plants should be watered for the first two years to get them established, and possibly during very dry periods if the plants show signs of stress.

Feeding

An annual application of a slow-release fertiliser will help, especially if the plant is pruned regularly as part of its maintenance.

Mulching

Maintain the mulch to a depth of 5–10cm (2–4in) by adding new material each year. This helps to reduce moisture loss from the soil and prohibit weed growth.

Pruning

This will vary depending on which plant is grown and its habit of growth. Some will require little or any pruning; others need annual pruning.

Weeding

Keep the area around the plant weed-free by hand weeding as required.

VERTICAL GARDENS

Vertical gardens can be fixed directly to the wall or they can be panels or sections that are either supported on a framework or freestanding. If fixed to the wall, ensure any irrigation water does not run down the wall, causing damp. Some are based on hydroponics; others use a growing media with an automatic watering system. They take up very little ground space but make good use of vertical space, so are very useful for small gardens and areas where plenty of vertical space is available.

A wide range of plants can be grown, from flowering and foliage to herbs, fruits and vegetables. Climbing plants can also be used to climb up or trail down. A whole wall of any size can be covered, or just sections of walls within easy reach. Unless the wall is shaded,

A colourful flowering and foliage display in a vertical wall. This will last all summer.

the plants will be in good light. The different aspects of the wall – north, south, east and west – give options for a range of plants on each wall. Vertical gardens help to protect the wall and cool the area and building by evapotranspiration in the summer, which will become more important as summers get warmer.

Building a Vertical Garden

There are different systems available, ranging from troughs that are fixed to the wall to plastic modules that are either fixed to the wall or a framework in front of the wall. Homemade vertical gardens can be made from pallets or other waste materials for a cheaper and more sustainable system.

This photograph shows a plastic trough system that can be fixed to a wall. This has been recently planted, but once established the plastic is covered by plants and is barely visible. The trough system has an automatic irrigation system, which feeds as well as waters, and the only maintenance required is trimming back and tidying the plants occasionally. After several years it may be necessary to remove and replace some of the plants if they start to die back with age – in a similar way to plants being removed and replaced in a garden.

The vertical wall container shown here is an example of a module system that can be fixed to the wall or framework and, again, watered automatically. Each module is planted up and once established forms a

A growing system for vertical walls, showing the fixings and plant growing containers that are watered from the top. Water trickles down to the bottom, from where it is recycled to the tank for future reuse.

densely planted wall cover, which looks very attractive. The module systems are also available for hydroponic growing, where plants are grown in a thin layer of water that trickles down from the top and is recycled and pumped back up.

Homemade vertical walls can be made from pallets stood on end and secured to a frame or wall. By fixing some extra slats across the pallet, growing shelves are made to hold the growing media; these are then planted up. Watering can be done by hand with a watering can or a semi-automatic system can be set up. They are useful for growing small vegetables like lettuce, as well as herbs and bedding plants.

If you have any wall space available, make use of it and grow some plants. They will improve the appearance of the wall or fence and make use of the space to absorb carbon dioxide. Growing some flowers or your own vegetables will also help you to overcome the cost-of-living crisis.

Eco-wall vertical wall system showing the individual troughs just after planting. Most of the containers will be hidden by plants once they are established.

Herbs growing in a vertical wall, giving both interest and a supply of herbs for culinary use.

RAIN GARDENS

This might seem an odd title for a section in this book, but rain gardens are likely to become more common in the future as they help to control the amount of water that can cause flooding. They have been used successfully in the US for several years. A rain garden comes into its own during heavy storms when flash flooding can be a problem – over the last five years these have become more frequent in the UK. Flash flooding is caused by the amount of rain not being able to enter the soil quickly enough but flooding off into roads, fields and other areas, causing damage to houses and other property. If the water flow can be slowed, it has more time to percolate into the soil and there is less water, if any, available to create floods.

Flooding is becoming a problem in major cities where many front gardens have been covered in hard landscaping like paving or tarmac, which means the rainwater runs off instead of percolating the soil. The London Fire Brigade had an exhibit at the 2022 Chelsea Flower Show to publicise the effects of flooding caused by rainstorms and flash flooding, which is creating extra problems and work for them. Large areas of roads, paving and other hard landscaping do not allow water to penetrate the ground, so the water runs off into the drains, often causing flooding further downstream.

The effects of climate change are likely to result in heavier downpours and storms where large amounts of rain fall in short periods and at a greater frequency.

Therefore, it is important that the water is directed into the soil rather than into drains, which cannot cope and overflow or runs off over hard surfaces, causing flooding. Rain gardens are useful to reduce local and even regional flooding, as well as creating an attractive area both to look at and for wildlife, therefore increasing biodiversity. They form part of a sustainable drainage system.

Small rain gardens can be incorporated into most gardens and bigger ones into open spaces and large gardens. A rain garden should form part of the overall garden design and not look as if it has just been added as an extra. They are basically shallow depressions in the ground of any shape or size, but they are usually sausage shaped and larger at one end than the other. Where possible, follow the contours of the land so that the water flows in the required direction and soaks into the soil. On sloping sites, the rain garden may cross the slope diagonally to slow the flow of water.

The base of the rain garden should be free draining; or materials such as gravel, crushed stone, broken hardcore, sand or similar can be incorporated in to improve the drainage. Tree prunings can be added, if they are available, as they help in water penetration – as they rot, they will absorb water. Bushes and prunings were used in the seventeenth century in some of the early field drains and worked well for many years.

The rain garden should be shaped to control and hold the flow of water. This can be achieved by raising the sides slightly, creating berms along each side and at the end. The depth and length of the rain garden will depend on the area it is receiving water from and the design of the garden – it should not be so deep that it dominates the garden. The rain garden should end with a slightly deeper depression that will hold water as it soaks into the soil; it may create a temporary mini pond like the dew ponds seen in fields years ago. Any water held in the rain garden is water that is not causing flooding further downstream.

Rain gardens can collect water from roof downpipes, areas of hard landscaping and surrounding ground. They need to be located so that they naturally collect the water, unless it can be piped to the rain garden.

The size of the rain garden will depend on the area available and the amount of rainfall it is expected to receive, which varies according to the area it is collected from (this can be calculated, as explained later). To avoid flooding your garden, the rain garden should be designed so that it overflows into an existing drainage system, pond, ditch or stream (permission is often required from the Environment Agency before diverting water into streams or rivers). Once the rainwater has entered the depression, it will percolate and drain through the soil; some will be held by the soil and organic matter and some used by the plants in the garden. In a heavy shower, the surplus will overflow into the drains, but this will only happen in severe rainstorms or if the soil is very wet after a wet winter.

Constructing a Rain Garden

Rain gardens should fall away from the house or other property in case they overflow and flood the building. Look at where the water would go if it overflowed – ideally into a drainage system (which can be an existing one or newly installed) or a pond. The rain garden inflow needs to be higher than the exit.

The size of the rain garden can be calculated by measuring the area it is to receive water from and multiplying this by an average rainfall of 15–20mm (½–¾in), which will cover most periods of rain we get in the UK and will accept a large proportion of any heavier storms. So, assuming a roof area of 100m² (109yd²) and rainfall of 15mm (½in), this will give a volume of 1.5m³ (5ft³) or 1,500 litres (330 gallons) of water. It is likely that a roof of that size would have three or four downpipes; if there are three downpipes there would be 500 litres (109 gallons) of water from each one, and this would easily be absorbed into most soils. A rough guide to the size is that the rain garden should be 20 to 25 per cent of the area it receives water from, assuming it has a depth of 15cm (6in) or more. Small rain gardens should be at least 1.5m (5ft) wide and 2–3m (6½–10ft) long; in larger areas they can be 3–5m (10–16½ft) wide with a length to suit the area it is collecting water from. If the rain garden is deeper than 15cm (6in), the area can be smaller, although the bigger the area the better as there is less chance of it overflowing.

The next consideration is the type of soil. Open sandy soils will absorb large amounts of water that will drain away relatively quickly, whereas a clay soil that is compacted will have a very slow percolation rate and is likely to become waterlogged quickly. Rain gardens can be constructed on clay soils; they just need ameliorating by digging to loosen them and adding stone, gravel or similar.

To check the drainage (percolation) rate, dig a hole in the proposed rain garden location to a depth of at least 30cm (12in, a spade's depth) and fill it with water. Allow the water to drain and then refill it; time the drainage rate and if it is 5cm (2in) an hour, the soil will be suitable. If it is slower than this, is the soil compacted? If so, break up the compaction and add some gravel, stone, crushed hardcore or similar to a depth of 0.5–1m (1.6–3¼ft). When the hole is dug, check to see if the water table is visible; if so, this will limit the amount of water the rain garden can absorb, especially in the winter when the water table can be high.

Rain gardens can be situated in existing lawns or borders, although these are likely to need modifying to work effectively. New rain gardens can be lawns, wildflower areas, borders or prairie planting; they can even grow fruit and vegetables if the right plants are chosen. They should blend into the existing or new design and form part of the overall arrangement. Ensure they do not overflow towards any property or into adjacent land. If the ground is sloping, check it is not too steep or water will tend to run down the rain garden and overflow before it has time to soak into the soil. A 10 per cent slope is the recommended maximum without relandscaping work to slow the flow, which can be done using swales (small shallow depressions that guide and control the flow of water, usually across a slope to slow the flow).

When ready to construct the rain garden, mark out the area using pegs, string, sand or spray can paint. Check it is in keeping with the area, and if possible, go upstairs and view it from a window. Dig out the area using hand tools for a small garden or a mini-digger or machinery for large rain gardens. Put any topsoil to one side and then grade out the base and sides to form gradual slopes and depressions, ending with a large saucer-shaped area. Soil dug out from the area is used to form berms around three sides of the rain garden, which helps to increase the amount of water it holds. Once happy with the size and shape, use the topsoil to cover the area for planting, grade to a gradual slope and prepare it for planting. As the berm will be holding back water, which can be heavy, the berms need to be 30–45cm (12–18in) wide. At the lowest point of the rain garden, place an overflow pipe or channel to direct any excess water to the drainage system, pond or ditch.

As mentioned earlier, if the soil is claylike or compacted this can be improved by loosening it when digging out the area and adding stone, gravel, crushed hardcore or similar materials – organic matter helps with the drainage of clay soils. If woody prunings are available, these can be incorporated as they help drainage and as they decompose they will absorb water.

The feed into the rain garden may just be a slope from the adjacent area it is draining, or channels in the ground covered with setts, stone or bricks to prevent soil erosion. If the water is coming from a roof or building, the water can be piped directly from a roof or existing downpipe.

Planting

Rain gardens can be planted up just as any other garden to be lawn or to include a wide range of plants. The plants chosen will depend on the soil type, location (sunny or shade) and garden design. As the soil may be wet for long periods, especially during the winter, it will pay to choose plants suitable for such conditions (*see* Chapter 7).

Maintenance

The rain garden will require the same maintenance as the rest of the garden, including weeding, deadheading, pruning and tidying up. There may be the occasional removal of silt or debris that can collect where water has run down a slope.

SWALES

Swales are used to divert and control the flow of water through a garden or over land. They are a shallow channel, often with a berm on either side. The water enters from one end and gradually flows along the swale. It then either soaks into the soil or gets to the end where it may run into a pond, ditch or rain garden. Where possible, the swale runs across a slope at an angle; in a large area of ground it may zigzag back and forth across the area. Swales are designed to reduce flooding and hold water onsite where it can be used by plants rather than run to waste off the site or into rivers, causing flooding further downstream.

Swales can be used to collect water from hard landscaped areas like car parks, roads or drives, or from roofs, overflows and sloping ground, where it could cause runoff and soil erosion. In a large area, several swales can be constructed and spaced 3–15m (3.3–16½yd) apart, running diagonally across the area. In large areas, small dams can be added to hold the water back and to create temporary ponds. The edges and berms of swales can be planted up with herbaceous plants and small shrubs.

CHAPTER 6

PERMACULTURE

Permaculture – short for permanent agriculture or permanent culture – was developed in Australia by David Holmgren and Bill Mollison. It is a system of growing that makes use of existing landforms and natural environments. It is ecologically sound, sustainable and based on natural systems, working *with* nature not against it. Permaculture offers practical solutions to some of the problems created by climate change and looks at how we should adapt not only to survive but to thrive. It does not just cover growing but life in general, and aspects like energy consumption, saving water, organic growing methods and the care of planet Earth and its people. We need to use everything to the optimum level and recycle all waste. Everything has a use and, in some cases, we just need to find it. Permaculturalists see solutions not problems.

The effects of climate change vary in different countries. In the UK we need to consider what our future problems are likely to be and how we can reduce them. We need to learn methods to adapt to overcome the effects of climate change by changing our growing habits, and permaculture is one way of doing this. Permaculturalists estimate that we could live our lives to the same standard but using only 40 per cent of our current energy consumption while also reducing our water consumption and recycling more of it – all things we seriously need to do.

Although permaculture originally started as a method of growing, over the years it has expanded into general living and the community as a whole and it looks at many aspects of living. It puts a big emphasis on recycling, both in the garden and house, to include nearly all forms of waste. In some of the more arid countries it considers all forms of water use as well as collecting and storing water. Although it does not claim to be organic, it follows most organic guidelines and minimises the use of chemicals, makes full use of organic matter and composting, and accepts both no-dig and digging as growing practices. Permaculture promotes 'grow your own' and recommends reducing the importation of food, especially from poorer countries that may be suffering from food shortages.

Growing local, even in cities, is widely promoted, and any spare land should be used for growing food or plants with other uses like herbs and timber. Areas need to be reafforested, which will increase the amount of carbon dioxide absorbed and also increase timber production, which is a sustainable and renewable resource. Trees have many functions, from reducing air pollution, noise and windspeed, providing shade and habitats for many creatures, and storing a vast amount of carbon. We need to become more self-reliant, which would help to make us less at the mercy of international crises, and also be energy efficient – not just in the garden but within the house and in our transport –making maximum use of renewable energy.

Too much time and effort is spent competing rather than achieving. Modern permaculture promotes cooperation rather than competition, as more can be achieved by cooperation than people competing, which is not always productive. We should plan for the long term not the short term, as many politicians do, which is how we end up having regular crises but achieve very little. Permaculture is about caring for the earth as well as caring for its people.

Before looking at the gardening side of permaculture I will just mention some of the other aspects that are followed by permaculturalists. Firstly it aims to prevent the loss of energy and nutrients offsite by turning them into cycles, so all plant waste is recycled by composting and returned to the soil. Wood is used for timber, firewood to heat the house and water and the ashes returned to the soil. Water is collected and stored not only for use in the garden but in the house as well for example flushing the toilet with rainwater or grey water. Sewerage is treated to produce organic matter for use on the land or even better humanure is produced (not everyone's choice!). The aim is to use everything at least once and fit into the cycles.

Aim to make maximum use of all incoming energy from the sun, rain (and other water like streams, rivers and lakes), wind, snow and waste. These can be used to create power, heat, irrigate plants and provide recycled materials. Reusing anything at least once will get the maximum energy out of it. Using the land efficiently is also part of getting the maximum use and energy out of it, so ground is never left empty but instead has a crop or green manure crop growing for the whole year.

Permaculture is not a single method of gardening but combines several techniques including polyculture, agroforestry, forest gardening, organic methods and other sustainable methods. We should consider the total yield from an area, not just the main (or possible only) crop. If we consider an orchard, the total yield can be the fruit, honey from pollination, a crop grown under the fruit trees, green manure grown in the rows between trees, or another crop and long-term possible timber for use as biomass. Other yields could be chickens or ducks allowed into the orchard to eat any pests and windfall fruit, or the windfalls fed to pigs, which eventually produce meat. The area between the trees can be planted up with perennial crops, bush fruits and shrubs.

DESIGNING A PERMACULTURE GARDEN

Permaculture starts with the design stage. Each element in the design will have many functions and we should try to make as many uses of it as possible. When including an element in a design, consider the functions, how these may affect its use in the design, and how they will be included. Taking a windbreak as an example, its functions could include reducing wind speed, providing firewood, providing timber like beanpoles or stakes, fodder for animal feed, fruit, nectar and pollen for bees and other insects, and, if capable of fixing nitrogen in its root, this will improve the amount of nitrogen available for later crops. The leaves from deciduous trees can be collected for leaf mould or left to be incorporated into the soil by worms. Underplanting a windbreak will provide shelter and vegetation for insects and other creatures, flowers and fruit, and the area can also be used by chickens, ducks or geese for grazing.

Whether starting with a new garden or an existing one, measure it up and note the size, shape and boundaries, as these are usually factors that cannot be changed, and then consider what you wish to include in the garden. List out all the elements such as a vegetable area, a herb garden, beehives, a compost area, fruit trees or an orchard (depending on the size of the garden), a pond and so on.

Zones

The next stage is to zone the garden, as the elements will be fitted into certain zones. The number of zones in a garden will depend on its size and what the gardener wishes to include. Most domestic gardens will have two to four zones, but large gardens or farms may have up to seven zones. The zones start from

Blackberry 'Chester' can be trained on wires and will grow in sun or part shade, giving a good crop of berries that are likely to need protecting from birds.

Allium proliferum (Egyptian Onions) – a perennial form of onions that can be divided each year.

Brassica oleracea var. *ramosa* (perennial kale) – one of the perennial Brassicas that have a long cropping period and are propagated by cuttings.

Rhubarb – a widely grown vegetable, used as a dessert. It will grow in full sun of partial shade. By growing a range of cultivars, rhubarb can be harvested from February to August.

the house, which is zone zero and the immediate surrounds are zone one, which is easy for access. The elements are placed into the appropriate zones and then the finer points of the design are considered.

Permaculture uses a range of plants, and not monocultures of plants like a field of wheat or carrots that makes the crop prone to pest and disease attacks. Aim to have a diversity of plants and crops, thus creating a polyculture. It makes use of many perennial crops, especially if they have a long cropping period or can be stored for later use, like top fruit. Many people have animals alongside plants, but this is up to individuals and they must work together harmoniously.

Zone Zero

Even the home can be used for growing – from mushrooms in the cellar or the cupboard under the stairs to sprouting seeds like mustard and cress grown on the windowsill. Even salad leaves can be grown in well-lit areas.

Zone One

Zone one is used for intensive vegetable growing, herbs, possibly a greenhouse and a compost heap. This area will be intensively planted and will have a very fertile, organic, rich soil that has been enriched with large amounts of organic matter and green manuring.

The size of zone one will depend on the amount of land available, which in modern houses is often fairly small. The thinking behind this is that the area of the garden that is likely to be visited the most is within easy distance to the house. This makes efficient use of time and is productive, as time is not wasted walking long distances down the garden to the vegetable plot.

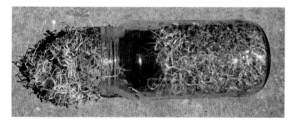

Sprouting seeds, ready to eat.

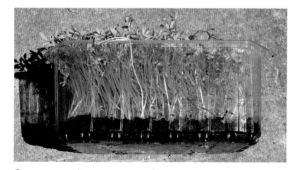

Cress, grown in a punnet, ready to eat.

Pea sprouts, grown in old margarine tubs and ready for the first harvest to be cut with scissors.

Although I must admit, many people would prefer to look out onto a flower garden or lawn than a vegetable patch!

Zone Two

This is the intensive fruit area, with chickens, a pond, windbreaks and perennial vegetables, if there is not room in zone one. This zone usually has a more informal layout than zone one and will include a wide range of plants – many, if not all, with multiple uses. There will be flowering plants for the benefit of pollinators; plants with edible leaves, fruit and flowers giving a large range of plants; and wide biodiversity.

Maintenance will be a lot lower than in zone one and the area may look semi-wild, but it will still provide a good yield. The perennial vegetables will be planted informally, not in rows or square blocks but to create a natural-looking landscape; they will be interplanted with fruit bushes and trees. Asparagus has attractive foliage; Jerusalem artichokes have nice sunflower-type flowers (to which it is related); and the globe artichoke has lovely light blue flowers. They are all quite tall (up to 2m/2¼yds), so fit in well with fruit, especially if on dwarfing rootstocks which control the size of the tree.

The soil below the trees and perennial vegetables is sown or planted with shade-loving plants to give a coverage of the soil, or sown to green manure to compost. If animals are included, chickens or ducks can be allowed to roam. A pond can be included for water storage, to provide a wildlife habitat and to give further biodiversity, including fish if desired.

Asparagus bed – a useful perennial crop giving a harvest from April to June.

Potager garden – a mix of flowers and vegetables giving an attractive appearance, some companion planting and harvest of crops.

Cynara cardunculus (Globe Artichoke) – a tall plant with grey foliage. Produces edible flower buds, which if not eaten give a colourful flower.

Zone Three

Zone three is the orchard, which can consist of tree fruits, small animals (if kept) and large ponds for fish or aquaculture. If bees are kept, the hives can be moved between zone three and zone two for fruit pollination. In small gardens, there may only be three zones and this zone could be the boundary area, so would include walls, fences and hedges. The walls and fences could have climbers or small fruit trees trained up them, with the hedges made up of fruiting species and other useful plants.

Gooseberry hedge with post and wire support. This acts as a hedge and produces fruit.

Zone Four

Finally, for medium- to large-sized areas, would be zone four, which includes woodland, livestock grazing, semi-managed areas, and other low intensively used or cropped areas.

Layers

When designing and planting the garden, consider the layering effect that is used in permaculture as opposed to monocultures that have just one layer: the crop layer. The aim is to have various layers like a woodland, which has the canopy layer, shrub layer, herbaceous layer, groundcover layer and edge plants.

The various layers make maximum use of the sunlight – some of which passes through the layers until it reaches the ground layer – and none is wasted. It is the same with rainwater, which passes through the crown of the trees and shrubs and then infiltrates into the soil and percolates down, being available to roots at all layers, so only the unused water drains away.

Although it is not feasible for small gardens to have all the layers, as large trees would be too big, they can still have three or four layers and can include small trees like apple and pear trees on a dwarf rootstock. By having layers and a range of species, a very good yield per area is achieved, as opposed to a single yield from a monoculture; yields can be improved by adding another layer if it is possible.

Canopy Layer

In a woodland, the canopy trees will be oak, ash, beech and other large trees; in a garden they could be any top fruit tree or small decorative trees like mountain ash (*Sorbus aucuparia*), small acers or small magnolias.

Shrub Layer

The shrub layer in a woodland would be, for example, elderberry, spindle tree or hazel; in a garden they could be bush fruit such as blackcurrant, redcurrant, white-currant and gooseberry. Included in the shrub layer are climbers. In a woodland these would be honeysuckle, brambles and ivy; in a garden they would include grape vines, cultivated blackberries, tayberries, loganberries and Japanese wineberries.

Herbaceous Layer

Woodland herbaceous plants include primulas, fox-glove and dogs' mercury. Gardens can contain a massive number of perennial plants, from perennial vegetables to the many perennial flowers.

Groundcover Layer

The groundcover plants in a woodland include ivy, mosses, lichens, fungi and similar very low-growing plants, some of which may be annuals. In the garden

Sorbus decora flowers in April or May and has berries in late August into autumn, so provides food for pollinating insects and birds.

Japanese wineberries, ready to harvest from late July to late August. Although the berries are small, they are tasty and produce a good yield in both sun and partial shade.

they can be low-growing perennials or annuals, but they need to have adapted to growing in shade.

Another layer are the root plants or xerophytes like the bulbs. In the woodland, these will include blue-bells, daffodils and snowdrops, which can all be grown in the garden, as can crocuses, tulips and scillas. These plants have adapted by coming out into leaf while the trees are dormant, growing and flowering before the trees are fully in leaf, making use of the winter light (energy).

Edge Effect

Edge plants are the plants that grow around the edge of a woodland, which has a higher light level than in the centre of the wood – this is the edge effect. They form a dense bank of foliage and will often produce good yields of fruit and flowers. The same edge effect can be seen around ponds, where there will be a wide range of species growing, forming a dense planting.

These plants have access to water and nutrients in the pond, good light levels and often very fertile soils, especially if the area has been flooded in the past, leaving deposits of silty soil. To make maximum use of the pond area, rather than having a round or oval pond it is better to have one with wavy or crenulated edges, as this creates a greater area for growing. The same is true of any edges such as woodlands, fruit areas or borders.

Things to Consider When Designing a Permaculture Garden

When designing the garden consider the following factors:

- Topography – If the ground is sloping, how steeply and in which direction (north, east, south or west)? This can affect the choice of plants to grow. If steeply sloping it could be prone to erosion so may need terracing or beds constructed.

- Soil type – Sand, silt, clay or the perfect loam we all dream about – this will affect the drainage and nutrient-holding capacity, the choice of plants and the work required to maintain a good soil. Soil pH will also affect the range of plants that can be grown.
- Wind – In which direction does the prevailing wind occur? Is the garden exposed or sheltered? Have there been any severe gales in recent years?
- Sunlight – Has the area a high sunlight level, like parts of the south coast of England, or a lower level? Higher light levels lead to more growth.
- Rainfall – With the likely effects of climate change, the annual rainfall level is going to be important. The western side of the UK is likely to continue having reasonably high rainfall, especially the northwest and Scotland. The eastern side will be drier and the southeast and East Anglia very dry, with the possibility of droughts in many years – saving water is going to be critical here. In dry areas instead of having raised beds, which can dry out quickly, dig out sunken beds that will catch, collect and store water for the plants.
- Water sources – Linked to the above is making use of any water sources to collect and store water, using gravity to collect, if possible. If not, use a pump, and if necessary pipe the water to a storage facility.

Permaculture aims to create edible ecosystems that are productive yet natural, using a minimum amount of energy and, where possible, no chemicals or artificial fertilisers – along similar lines to organic growing. It grows a diverse range of plants in layers (also called stacking in permaculture), which – although each type of plant may not yield highly – the total yield from the area will be equal if not higher than conventional growing.

We need to reduce our consumption of non-renewable resources and make better use of renewable resources like timber, energy and water. We need to leave a healthy planet for future generations and to grow more food in cities and other urban areas, making better use of parks, verges, open spaces and waste ground. Permaculture is not just a way of growing plants and rearing animals but a sustainable way of living, covering energy use, water, waste reduction and recycling, but also creating a very diverse landscape, which is required if we are to overcome the problems created by climate change.

FOREST GARDENS

Forest gardens are a separate method of growing to permaculture but fit very well into it, and many people consider it to be part of permaculture. It uses permaculture principles, such as layers and making full use of the soil, growing a range of perennial plants, mainly trees and shrubs. The actual growing is similar to permaculture and the aim is to make full use of the various plant layers from the crown of a tree, through the shrub and herbaceous layers to the lower-growing groundcover plants. Forest gardens have become better known following books by Robert Hart and more recently Martin Crawford. If space is available, it is a method of growing that is both sustainable and suitable in likely future climatic conditions.

To have a 'full' forest garden needs a reasonable area of ground – more than is available in most modern semi-detached gardens – but it is still possible to make use of some of the principles and grow some of the plants, even in small gardens. Some of the plants have an ornamental value and look attractive, especially when in flower.

One of the reasons for considering forest gardens when adapting for climate change is that many of the plants grown are perennial and, apart from when planting, the soil is kept covered thus helping to prevent soil erosion. Because forest gardens tend to have layers of plants, this protects the soil and reduces the amount of rain entering it, which is held in place by the plant roots; all this helps to reduce flooding and maintain soil fertility.

Designing a Forest Garden

When designing any garden, full use should be made of all the layers to provide year-round interest. Over a year, the trees, shrubs, herbaceous plants and groundcover can all flower; some may have colourful leaves or stems followed by autumn colour and many will produce edible leaves or fruit. An advantage for the less keen gardener is there is very little weeding, other than the removal of unwanted brambles and strimming other unwanted growth.

To create a full-sized forest garden needs an area of a couple of acres (nearly a hectare) of land. However, a mini forest garden can be created in a corner or small area of a garden by planting top fruit, like apples, pears, cherries or plums with close-by bush or cane fruit like raspberries, blackcurrants or gooseberries, and the area underplanted with strawberries or perennial vegetables that will grow in some shade. Although the yields from the underplanting will be lower than if grown in the open in full sunlight, the overall yield from the area will be higher as there are three crops in the same area.

For a forest garden to work, the plants need to be carefully chosen to grow in the conditions provided and be compatible with the other adjacent plants. Higher yielding annual vegetables are better grown in a separate area.

Advantages of a Forest Garden

A good forest garden will look a bit like an open woodland (hence the name), with a range of different plants, mainly perennials like trees and shrubs. Unlike an orchard, which tends to have one type of fruit like apples or pears; a forest garden is a mix of different species of tree, which can be planted in groups of the same species or cultivars, this being useful for pollination.

Over time, a forest garden can become quite fertile as much of the leaves and other plant debris (organic matter) is returned to the soil and is incorporated by the various soil fauna like earthworms. If using nitrogen-fixing plants like legumes, which are capable of absorbing nitrogen from the air and using it for growth, when these die, the nitrogen is added to the soil for future plants. The fact that the soil is covered with vegetation also improves its fertility.

Another advantage of forest gardens is that they attract a wide range of wildlife, resulting in a more biodiverse garden, which is badly needed these days with many insect species getting close to extinction. Forest gardens are low maintenance and have a low energy requirement, as well as being productive, producing a wide range of crops from fruit and nuts to vegetables, herbs, salads and mushrooms.

HÜGELKULTUR BEDS

Hügelkultur is a German word meaning hill or mound culture, and a hügelkultur bed is basically a raised bed for growing plants, whether it be vegetables, fruits, herbs or flowers. These were developed in Europe and have a number of uses.

Hügelkultur beds are well worth considering in new gardens where the builders have left very poor-quality soil and often a load of rubbish. Any hardcore could be used for paths or go into the bottom of the hügelkultur and all green waste (except perennial weeds' roots, which need killing first by either drying or soaking in water for a few weeks) used to build it. I hope to see more of them in the future.

Advantages of Hügelkultur Beds

The advantages of hügelkultur beds are that they often make good use of waste organic material, giving a greater surface area for growing plants compared to a flat area and creating different growing aspects. They can be used to control and reduce the flow of water, providing a fertile growing soil. On wet or even waterlogged ground, plants can be grown on hügelkultur beds as they are above the wet soil and drain well, even though they absorb water. Hügelkultur beds are a very good method of sequestering carbon into the soil and are worth building for this reason alone.

Building a Hügelkultur Bed

A Hügelkultur bed may not fit into everyone's gardens and might not be to everyone's taste but they are useful in some gardens. They can be built on the existing ground or a trench, a spade or more in depth, can be dug out and the soil put to one side.

On sloping ground, build across or diagonally across the slope – this helps to control and slow the flow of water; they work very well as swales as they both direct and absorb water. Next any woody waste from twigs, branches or even tree trunks is stacked in the bottom (this is a very good method of disposing of woody prunings and other tree and shrub waste). Firm the wood waste into position by standing on it, then cover with some of the soil dug out or use any other available soil, even if of poor quality. Cover this with a layer of thinner woody waste, small prunings, weeds, straw, leaves, leaf mould, cabbage stumps, cardboard, paper and other organic waste that could be composted; once a thick layer has been formed, cover with soil again. This can be repeated until the required height is achieved, when the hügelkultur is covered with the final layer of soil, or rotted compost if soil is not available. A layer of 15cm (6in) is useful as this gives the seeds and plants something to get established into and grow; but less can be used if not available. If constructing more than one hügelkultur, the soil from the paths between them can be used to help construct and cover them.

There is no set height, width of length of a hügelkultur bed – they can be any length but are best if not too long as you have to walk around them to get to the other side for working and harvesting. The width is to some extent dictated by the height, as the taller the bed is, the wider it needs to be to prevent it sliding down. Any height between 60cm (24in) up to 2m (2¼yd) have been built with widths of 90cm (35in) to 1.5m (5ft); the bigger they are, the more waste can be used and the larger the growing area.

Maintaining a Hügelkultur Bed

Over time, the organic matter in the hügelkultur decomposes and it settles to a lower height. It can be left at this height or topped up as required, especially if you have more woody waste to dispose of. As the material decomposes this produces a fertile growing media that holds moisture, giving a very good growing environment. The angle of the sides does not matter as long as they are stable and do not slide down; stakes or small straight branches can be hammered into the sides if required but they are not usually used unless the sides are very steep.

As the wood and green waste decompose, there is a gradual release of nutrients and the wood starts to

Hügelkultur bed, planted with nasturtiums.

hold water as it rots, meaning watering is not often required after the first year. The rotted wood acts as a sponge and will hold a good amount of water. After the first year, hügelkultur beds rarely need watering unless in a severe drought and they have an overall low water requirement; again, good for climate change.

If the mound is high in woody material in the first year, there may be a slight nitrogen shortage as the bacteria that break down the wood use the nitrogen to balance the high carbon level. A light application of a nitrogen fertiliser will overcome this problem and is only required during the first year.

The hügelkultur beds can be sown or planted with any vegetables and in a south-facing slope will be ideal for tomatoes and other crops that like a warmer environment. Any fruit will grow and crop – these are planted after the bed has settled a bit (leave six to eight weeks, if possible) and will be a permanent planting. Herbs grow well, but are better near the top of the mound where it is free draining and drier, which most herbs prefer. A decorative mound can be planted up with annual or perennial flowers or shrubs for a permanent border; they can also be sown with wildflower or meadow mixtures. If at any time the hügelkultur bed is empty, sow it with green manure seeds, allow them to grow and then harvest and compost the material when the bed is wanted or the green manure is ready. It makes good use of the area and helps to prevent erosion of the sides.

CHAPTER 7

CHOOSING PLANTS

As the effects of climate change become more pronounced, it is likely that plants will have to survive not only droughts but also very wet conditions or even flooding, especially during the autumn and winter. There is also predicted to be an increase in severe storms, which will cause damage not only to plants but also to property. It is not too difficult to find drought-tolerant plants, as many plants have evolved to grow in these conditions – cacti and succulents being good examples. However, there are very few parts of the world that have droughts and floods regularly; the dry parts of the world tend to be dry, like the Mediterranean countries, where flooding is rare and short-lived. If drought-tolerant plant roots are sat in water for any length of time, they will soon die, even if it is not waterlogged, as they have not evolved for these conditions.

Choose plants that will grow in the natural conditions of the site. Note the soil type, pH, structure, and condition; also consider the microclimate of the site, available light or shade, amount of shelter, whether it is open and exposed, and any other factors that could affect plant growth. If the soil has an acid pH, use plants that grow in this type of soil, which saves having to keep modifying the pH at regular intervals.

Plant adaptations like hairy leaves are very good in hot dry summers, but in cold wet winters the same leaves can soon rot, owing to the moisture on the leaves, resulting in plant death. It is necessary to choose plants that will survive or, even better, thrive in the range of climatic conditions that we are likely to experience in the future.

Trees like beech have a shallow root system, making them prone to blowing over in stormy weather and they are not very tolerant of wet, heavy soils. Hornbeam, which has similar leaves to beech, has a deeper root system and will thrive in wet claylike soils, so will be a better choice. Beech, owing to its shallow root system, is also susceptible to drought so is likely to be less successful in the south of the UK in the future. It all comes down to right plant, right place.

CARBON SEQUESTRATION

Plants can help to reduce the high carbon dioxide levels in the atmosphere by absorbing CO_2 as part of the photosynthesis process. If enough plants are grown, this could help reduce the CO_2 levels to a safer level for the future. Trees, shrubs and the soil will store carbon for the long term, especially if permanent plantings and grown using minimum cultivations. It may not make a massive difference but every little counts.

We need to increase carbon sequestration using both plants and the soil (see Chapter 2). Trees are the main plants to absorb carbon in reasonable quantities; it is stored in the lignin (woody tissue). Young trees between ten to fifty years old store the maximum amount of carbon as they are growing fast, but they will absorb and store carbon for most of their lives. Planting trees as part of vegetation layers so that each layer absorbs carbon dioxide increases the amount absorbed per area of ground as well as creating a more biodiverse ecosystem. It is important to encourage dense planting and growth to absorb carbon, protect the soil and reduce some of the effects of climate change.

Planting in layers makes full use of the vertical environment as each layer provides interest and habitats for creatures. The top layer is the tree canopies, below these are the smaller trees and shrubs, under which grow the herbaceous plants and finally the ground-cover plants – very similar to an open woodland. Having layers also protects the soil from erosion and damage by heavy rain.

Shrubs and hedges also absorb useful amounts of carbon dioxide; the larger the plants, the more they absorb and store. Hedges are a more sustainable boundary in the future compared to fences that rot and are prone to blowing down, especially in stormy weather – of which we are likely to see more as climate change progresses. Hedges also act as very good windbreaks as they filter the wind, reducing its speed and resulting in less damage in the garden, as opposed to fences and walls which tend to cause turbulence, resulting in more damage.

Using perennial plants and crops helps to sequester carbon, and techniques like forest gardening, agroforestry and polycultures (mixed crops rather than monocrops) all also absorb useful amounts of carbon.

PLANTS FOR DROUGHT

With climate change, many plants that were considered to be tender and not survive outdoors in the UK during the winter will now not only survive the winter conditions but also thrive in the new climate, which is more to their liking. This is partly owing to the warmer summers but also the less severe winters with fewer and shorter cold spells. This saves moving the plants to the greenhouse or conservatory over winter as they can be left as part of the permanent planting.

Many of the plants that grow and often thrive in drought conditions have adapted or evolved to grow in these conditions and will be native to some of the drier areas of the world, including the Mediterranean countries, California, the Middle East, Australia and parts of South America. Plants that have adapted to grow in these conditions are often very efficient in using water. Many will have good deep root systems, usually with a tap root, which can obtain water from the lower depths of the soil. Other adaptations include waxy outer skin coverings, very hairy leaves, small leaves or even no leaves – some like the conifers have needlelike or scalelike leaves – these all reduce the water loss from the leaf, enabling the plant to survive even during prolonged droughts.

Some plants roll their leaves into a tube shape, with the stomata on the inside, reducing water loss; grasses, like some of the fescues, are typical examples. Alternatively, the top surface of the leaf curls under at the edges, like rosemary, or the leaves are reduced in size. In extreme examples, many cacti do not have leaves or the stomata only open at night when it is cooler, again reducing water loss. Some plants that have adapted to drought conditions have become very efficient at using water and have waxy coverings to reduce loss.

To help in choosing suitable plants we will look at some of the adaptations in more detail, so you know the types of plants to use in dry areas.

Plant Adaptations

Plants have evolved over thousands of years to grow in the conditions of their native habitat.

Succulent or Fleshy Foliage

These plants are often called succulents and have thick fleshy leaves often covered in a grey waxy bloom, which reflects sunlight, and a thick waxy cuticle to conserve water. These plants include sedums, agave, aloe, yucca, *Hylotelephium* and cacti.

Aloe polyphylla – a typical succulent. Its waxy grey leaves have a sharp point to prevent herbivores eating them.

Plectranthus 'Silver Shield' has grey hairy leaves, giving good drought resistance and an attractive appearance. It can be used in bedding and containers.

Hylotelephium spectabile 'Indian Chief' – an excellent late summer-flowering succulent.

Thick Epidermis

This thick skin reduces water loss, even in hot sunny weather. Typical plants include rosemary, *Ceanothus*, laurel and many cacti.

Hairy or Woolly Leaves

Very short hairs help to reduce water loss as they reduce the temperature of the leaf by reflecting some of the sunlight. They also slow the speed of evaporation from the leaf as they reduce the effect wind has on the leaf surface. Typical plants with woolly or hairy leaves are *Stachys byzantina*, *Phlomis fruticosa*, *Salvia officinalis*, *Ballota pseudodictamnus* and *Plectranthus* 'Silver Shield'.

Santolina incana – a small grey-leaved shrub with yellow flowers in the summer, ideal for the front of borders and sunny beds. The leaves are scented if crushed.

Leaf Size

Smaller leaves will have a lower water loss than larger ones, as they have less surface area from which to lose water. Plants with small leaves include thymes, *Helianthemums*, *Dianthus* and some *Ceanothus*; others like rosemary (now called *Salvia rosmarinus*) have narrow leaves.

Needlelike or Scalelike Leaves

Conifers have evolved either needlelike or scalelike leaves, which have a thick epidermis or waxy covering as well as being thin, allowing wind to pass through without causing much damage. They have evolved these leaves to survive and grow in very inhospitable climates, often at higher altitudes or in very cold areas like the Arctic or Siberia. These areas have bright sunlight during the summer but are usually cold and windy in the winter, especially at high altitudes.

Many needles are rolled inwards along their length with the stomata on the inside, which reduces water loss. Plants with needles are pines, firs and spruces, and those with scalelike leaves include Leyland cypress, Lawsons cypress, Cupressus and some junipers.

Picea glauca 'Alberta Blue Haal' – a small blue-grey conifer, suitable for small gardens, giving year-round interest.

Grey Waxy Leaves

The grey colour helps to reflect sunlight, keeping the leaf cooler. The waxy covering reduces water loss from the leaf. Examples include *Euphorbia characias* subsp. 'Wulfenii' and *Dianthus*.

Deep Root Systems

These tap-like roots can penetrate deep into the soil, possibly down to the water table or at least into soil that very rarely dries out. Good examples in the UK are dandelion and dock weeds, which usually stay green long after the lawn has gone brown.

Trees are often considered to have deep root systems, but considering the size of the plant this is not often the case, and even a very large tree may only have a root system that penetrates 60–90cm (24–35in). Therefore, when choosing trees, choose species from warmer climates or those that have adapted to dry conditions.

Producing Seeds Early

Some annuals that flower in early summer produce their seeds and die before any drought becomes fully established, which affects the plants' life cycles. The

Cupressus arizonica var. *glauca* 'Blue Ice' – a conifer with narrow foliage and a grey colour that reflects the sunlight.

Chamaerops humilis var. *argentea* – a tropical-looking plant with silvery-white foliage to reflect strong sunlight. It gives character to borders.

seeds then germinate when the winter rains arrive, and the plants grow quickly to flowering size. This can be used to our advantage by sowing hardy annuals in the autumn to overwinter and then flower in early summer before a drought becomes severe.

Perennating Organs

These include the bulbs, tubers, corms and rhizomes, which store both food and water, sometimes to survive overwinter but, in some cases, to survive hot dry summers. Many tulips are native to the Middle East and grow and flower in the late winter or spring, then die down in the summer when it is hot and dry. Most of the spring flowering bulbs have grown, flowered and died down by the summer when any drought takes effect.

Low-growing Plants

One of the ways that alpines have adapted to survive in cold mountainous climates is by being low-growing, which allows most of the wind to blow over them without causing any damage. Plants with a height of only 15–20cm (6–8in) are unlikely to be badly damaged by wind. These plants have also evolved to be rounded or hummock-shaped, which tends to deflect the wind away.

Plant Shape

As well as being low and rounded, some plants have evolved an open habit that allows wind to pass through rather than cause damage; *Cornus alba* being a good example. Trees like silver birch (*Betula pendula*) and weeping willow (*Salix babylonica*) have twigs that move with the wind, thus reducing damage. Although willow has a brittle wood, it is usually only the twig ends that break off, and these often root where they land!

WIND DAMAGE

Climate change is likely to result in more storms and high winds that will damage plants. Once damaged, the plant is open to attack by diseases that usually enter via wounds. Storms damage plants by blowing leaves off, which may not be a problem in the autumn but it is during the summer as it reduces the rate of photosynthesis and therefore the growth of the plant. High winds increase the rate of transpiration and therefore water loss. Very cold winds in the winter can also scorch some leaves, which reduces plant growth, and it can take the plant some months to recover.

To reduce the effects of wind damage, firstly consider from which direction the main winds will come – usually the southwest in the UK, although some of the more damaging winds can come from other directions, like the 'Beast from the East'! The wind direction can also depend on the local topography – winds can blow along valleys, or large obstructions like tall buildings or hills can affect the direction of the wind and create turbulence, which is even more damaging. It is impossible to stop the wind, but is possible to reduce it by using windbreaks or shelterbelts.

Windbreaks

Windbreaks can be artificial or planted and should be erected or planted across the direction of the wind (at 90 degrees to the wind). A good windbreak is 50 per cent permeable to the wind and filters the wind, rather than stopping it.

If walls or solid fences are used, they will create turbulence, which results in the windspeed increasing in the areas adjacent to the wall or fence. Instead of walls, use windbreak material that allows half of the wind to pass through but the speed to be reduced – this is usually sufficient to prevent any plant damage. Windbreak materials include Rokolene, Tildenet, Paraweb and others. They range in height from 1–3m (1–3¼yd) and come In rolls, which are cut to length. They should be fixed to solid posts of good timber or concrete, set well in the ground. They take up little space and will last a number of years before needing replacement, or a hedge or shelterbelt has grown to the required size.

Using Plants

An alternative to artificial windbreaks is to use plants; this can be as simple as a hedge or a number or rows of plants. Hedges work very well and can be allowed to grow to the height required to give maximum shelter from the wind. Hedges allow some of the wind to pass through, but not all – this gives good shelter to any plants on the leeward side.

The following plants are suitable for hedges:

- Beech (*Fagus sylvatica*)
- Hornbeam (*Carpinus betulus*)
- Hawthorn (*Crataegus monogyna*)
- *Photinia* × *fraseri* 'Red Robin'
- Common yew (*Taxus baccata*)

Shelterbelts

On larger sites, shelterbelts can be planted. These are a lot wider than hedges and need a reasonable amount of land to grow well. They consist of five to ten rows (there can be more if required) of plants, planted in staggered rows, usually of mixed species, and can include pines, firs, beech, hornbeam, field maple and Norway maple, as well as some shrubs to form the lower planting.

Other Methods of Reducing Wind

Pleached Trees

This is like a hedge on stilts that acts as a very good screen, both to reduce the wind but also to screen unsightly structures outside of the garden. Each plant has a trunk with a two-dimensional flat crown that is trained horizontally to form a hedge-like appearance. They do not take up a lot of space, look attractive and form a good windbreak.

Trellis and Lath Fencing

These are not a solid barrier, so allow some of the wind through. Plants can also be trained up them to add interest and colour. After time, the supporting posts can rot so need replacing.

Good Climbing Plants

- **Ivy *(Hedera)*** Ivies are evergreen and there are a wide range of different species and cultivars in large- and small-leaved as well as dark green and variegated forms. They are self-clinging, and despite the myths they do not harm good walls, if the wall is in poor condition they will cling to loose material that will come away if the ivy is removed. Ivy forms a very good insulating layer over the wall. *Hedera helix* is the small-leaved ivy, with many types available; *Hedera canariensis* and *Hedera colchica* are larger leaved.
- ***Hydrangea anomala* subsp. *Petiolaris*** The climbing hydrangea grows well on north walls and produces white flowers. It will cling to the wall or fence, but is better if given a few wires for support.
- ***Parthenocissus*** – rampant climbers with good autumn colours. The main species grown are *henryana* and *quinquefolia*, the Virginia creepers, and *tricuspidata*, the Boston ivy.
- ***Actinidia kolomikta*** – again, fairly rampant but worth growing for its pink, white and green leaves, which give it an attractive appearance that stands out on the wall. It needs a support to twine around.
- ***Humulus lupulus* 'Aureus'** – has excellent bright yellow foliage all summer and will twine around any supports. It stands out in the border or garden.

Dead Hedge or Fedge

See Chapter 1. The height of these will depend on the size of the garden to be protected and the effect they will create. A tall hedge may be overpowering and dominate the garden, as well as casting too much shade (think the High Hedges Act and all the overtall Leyland Cypresses).

SUCCULENTS

Cacti and succulents grow in many arid areas in the world and are native from North America down to Chile and Argentina, as well as from North Africa to South Africa, which has a different range of species. They have evolved to grow in hot dry climates with low levels of rain, and some can be quite cold at night. Species that grow in mountainous or cold areas are likely to be reasonably hardy in the UK and are well worth a try.

Succulents survive by storing water in their leaves or stems, which usually have a waxy covering. In the UK they are happy in full sun and can tolerate temperatures down to -5°C, as long as it is dry and they do not thaw too quickly, as this is when cell damage is caused. They dislike wet winters, which are more likely to kill them than the cold, when they can easily be protected by a fleece covering.

The ideal area would be a sunny south-facing slope with a soil that is free draining and some shelter from the worst of the winter weather; but this varies depending on the part of the country they are in. In the southern half of the UK, with the effects of climate change it is likely that they will survive in most locations, with the exceptions of really wet areas and frost pockets. If the soil is claylike they grow well in containers, especially clay or terracotta pots, which tend to be drier than plastic pots. If grown in containers, a soil-based growing media like John Innes potting compost is better than peat or peat-free media.

Whichever compost is used, add some grit, coarse sand or gravel to improve the drainage and add weight to the container for stability. Water as required during the summer, just letting the compost dry out before watering, but keep dry over winter – they should not need watering from October to March. Feed with liquid feed once a fortnight to once a month with half-strength solution.

If planting out, do not plant too deep and mulch with gravel or chippings. Prepare the soil by adding stone, gravel or coarse sand, if required. If the soil is claylike, add some organic matter to open up the structure.

Plants for Drought Conditions

Succulents

- *Aeonium arboreum* and 'Atropurpureum', aeonium 'Zwartkop'
- *Agave filifera*, *A. gracilipes*, *A. scabra*, *A. palmeri*, *A. americana* and 'Variegata', *A. americana* 'Mediopicta' and 'Alba', *A. parryi*, *A. montana*
- *Aloe arborescens*, *A. aristata*, *A. ferox*, *A. striatula*
- *Beschorneria yuccoides*
- *Billbergia nutans*
- *Carpobrotus edulis*
- *Delosperma cooperi*, *D. nubigenum*
- *Dorotheanthus bellidiformis*
- *Echeveria elegans*, *E. glauca*
- *Echinocereus cinerascens*, *E. pentalophus*
- *Euphorbia resinifera*
- *Graptopetalum paraguayensis*
- *Lampranthus spectabilis*
- *Lewisia cotyledon*
- *Mammillaria magnimamma*, *M. karwinskiana*, *M. polythele*
- *Opuntia engelmannii*, *O. humifusa*
- *Puya alpestris*
- *Sedum acre* and 'Aureum', *S. cauticola*, *S. spathulifolium*, *S. spectabile* and cultivars
- *Sempervivum arachnoideum*, *S. montanum*, *S. tectorum*
- *Yucca baileyi*, *Y. elata*, *Y. filamentosa*, *Y. gloriosa*, *Y. pallida*, *Y. recurvifolia*

Climbers and Wall Shrubs

These plants will grow up walls, fences or other vertical surfaces. Some will need support, like wires or trellis; others are self-supporting.

- *Actinidia arguta*
- *Actinidia deliciosa*
- *Actinidia kolomikta*
- *Akebia quinata*
- *Argyrocytisus battandieri*
- *Campsis radicans*
- *Clematis cirrhosa*
- *Clematis montana* and other species/cultivars
- *Cobaea scandens*

- *Euonymus fortunei* var. *radicans*
- *Fallopia baldschuanica*
- *Fremontodendron* 'California Glory'
- *Hedera canariensis*
- *Hedera colchica* 'Dentata'
- *Hedera helix*
- *Humulus lupulus* 'Aureus'
- *Hydrangea petiolaris*
- *Lonicera japonica*
- *Parthenocissus henryana*
- *Parthenocissus quinquefolia*
- *Parthenocissus tricuspidata*
- *Passiflora caerulea*
- *Solanum crispum* 'Glasnevin'
- *Solanum jasminoides* 'Album'
- *Trachelospermum jasminoides*
- *Vitis coignetiae*
- *Vitis vinifera*
- *Wisteria sinensis*
- × *Fatshedera lizei*
- × *Fatshedera lizei* 'Variegata'

Annuals

These plants will need sowing each year, unless they self-seed the previous year.

- *Amaranthus caudatus*
- *Calendula officinalis*
- *Centaurea cyanus*
- *Cerinthe major*
- *Cleome hassleriana*
- *Cosmos bipinnatus*
- *Echium vulgare*
- *Eschscholzia californica*
- *Helianthus annuus*
- *Limnanthes douglasii*
- *Mesembryanthemum bellidiformis*
- *Nigella damascena*
- *Papaver rhoeas*
- *Portulaca grandiflora*
- *Zinnia elegans*

Bulbs

- Agapanthus species/cultivars
- *Allium cristophii*

- *Allium hollandicum*
- *Allium moly*
- *Allium sphaerocephalon*
- *Allium tuberosum*
- *Asphodeline lutea*
- *Cyclamen hederifolium*
- *Galanthus nivalis*
- *Muscari armeniacum* and *M. neglectum*
- *Narcissus papyraceus*
- *Scilla peruviana*

Grasses

- *Briza media*
- *Calamagrostis* × *acutiflora* 'Karl Foerster'
- *Cortaderia selloana*
- *Deschampsia* species
- *Festuca glauca* 'Elijah Blue'
- *Hakonechloa macra*
- *Lagurus ovatus*
- *Miscanthus sinensis* 'Ferner Osten'
- *Miscanthus sinensis* 'Zebrinus'
- *Pennisetum alopecuroides*
- *Stipa tenuissima*

Palms

- *Chamaerops humilis*
- *Cordyline australis*
- *Trachycarpus fortunei*

Herbaceous Perennials

- *Acanthus mollis*
- *Acanthus spinosus*
- *Achillea millefolium* and cultivars
- *Agastache foeniculum*
- *Alchemilla mollis*
- *Artemisia absinthium*
- *Ballota pseudodictamnus*
- *Bergenia cordifolia* and cultivars
- *Calamintha nepeta*
- *Centranthus ruber*
- *Convolvulus cneorum*
- *Crambe maritima*

- *Crocosmia* 'Lucifer'
- *Dianella tasmanica*
- *Echinops ritro*
- *Erigeron karvinskianus*
- *Eryngium agavifolium*
- *Eryngium bourgatii*
- *Eryngium giganteum*
- *Eryngium* × *zabelii*
- *Euphorbia amygdaloides* var. *robbiae*
- *Euphorbia characias* subsp. *wulfenii*
- *Foeniculum vulgare*
- *Geranium macrorrhizum*
- *Geranium sanguineum*
- *Iris germanica*
- *Kniphofia* species and cultivars
- *Liriope muscari*
- *Lychnis coronaria*
- *Melianthus major*
- *Nepeta* × *faassenii*
- *Ophiopogon planiscapus* 'Kokuryu'
- *Oenothera lindheimeri*
- *Salvia sclarea*
- *Sisyrinchium striatum*
- *Stachys byzantina*
- *Verbena bonariensis*

- *Helichrysum italicum*
- *Jacobaea maritima*
- *Lavendula angustifolia*
- *Lavandula stoechas*
- *Myrtus communis*
- *Nandina domestica*
- *Nerium oleander*
- *Olearia macrodonta*
- *Phlomis russeliana*
- *Phormium tenax* and cultivars
- *Pittosporum tenuifolium* and cultivars
- *Punica granatum*
- *Rhamnus alaternus* 'Argenteovariegata'
- *Romneya coulteri*
- *Salvia* 'Blue Spire'
- *Salvia officinalis*
- *Salvia rosmarinus*
- *Santolina chamaecyparissus*
- *Teucrium chamaedrys*
- *Teucrium fruticans*
- *Thymus vulgaris* and other species and cultivars
- *Ugni molinae*
- *Vitex agnus-castus*
- *Zauschneria californica*

Shrubs

- *Abelia* species
- *Brachyglottis* 'Sunshine'
- *Buddleja alternifolia*
- *Buddleja davidii*
- *Buddleja globosa*
- *Bupleurum fruticosum*
- *Carpenteria californica*
- *Caryopteris* × *clandonensis*
- *Ceratostigma plumbaginoides*
- *Ceratostigma willmottianum*
- *Cistus* × *purpureus*
- *Cytisus* species
- *Eriobotrya japonica*
- *Ficus carica*
- *Genista aetnensis*
- *Genista lydia*
- *Griselinia littoralis*
- *Hebe* species

Ferns

- *Asplenium scolopendrium*
- *Dryopteris filix-mas* 'Cristata'
- *Polypodium vulgare*
- *Polystichum setiferum*

Trees

- *Acacia dealbata*
- *Acca sellowiana*
- *Albizia julibrissin*
- *Cercis siliquastrum*
- *Cupressus sempervirens*
- *Eucalyptus pauciflora* subsp. *Niphophila*
- *Laurus nobilis*
- *Olea europaea*
- *Quercus ilex*
- *Quercus suber*

CHAPTER 8

PLANT DIRECTORY

The plant directory gives brief details and a photograph of a range of plants that are likely to be suitable for growing in the UK and similar climates in the future as climate change progresses. The photographs show the type of plant, habit of growth and some of the colours available.

There is a good choice of plants suitable for dry sites and drought conditions, as well as some that will prefer a damper soil, which will be suitable for the wetter western side of the UK.

Most of the plants are widely available from nurseries or garden centres, or if difficult to find, suppliers are listed in the latest edition of the *RHS Plant Finder* book (published every year) or on the RHS website in the 'Find a Plant' section, by searching for the plants you want.

Acaena microphylla (New Zealand Bur)

A very low-growing evergreen perennial, only 5–10cm (2–4in) tall and spreading 20–30cm (8–12in). *Acaena* is native to New Zealand, where many drought-tolerant plants originate. It is grown mainly for its foliage colour as its small leaves are tinged with bronze. Although

Acaena saccaticupula 'Blue Haze' gives a nice blue colour to the front of the border.

some species flower, it tends to be the bracts that stand out, giving the plant a brownish appearance over winter. It is happy in full sun and part shade, will grow on most soils and is used as a substitute for grass in non-grass lawn areas or low groundcover. Propagation is by division in autumn or spring.

Achillea millefolium (Yarrow)

A herbaceous perennial, useful in borders and wild-flower areas as well as being a weed in lawns. The height varies depending on the cultivar chosen and its habitat, but most are between 30cm (12in) and 1m (3¼ft) tall. *Achillea* has a wide colour range, from white or yellow to pastel shades, with a long flowering period starting in midsummer; they are also suitable for drying

for indoor displays. The foliage is fernlike and contrasts well with other larger leaved perennials. *Achillea* grows in most soils in full sun or part shade and is a plant that will tolerate drought, having a good root system and reasonably small leaf area. Propagation is by division or seed for the common species and newer cultivars.

Agapanthus (African Lily)

There are many cultivars and species available of *Agapanthus* with a colour range of white, light blue and dark blue. They mainly originate from South Africa, so are used to dry climates and prefer a dry free-draining soil and sunny position; they are also very good in containers. The plants form clumps of strap-like foliage with straight flower stems topped with

Achillea millefolium 'Moonshine'.

Agapanthus 'Northern Star'.

Achillea ptarmica 'Summer Pastels Group'.

Agapanthus 'Queen Mother'.

bell-shaped flowers. With the effects of climate change and the newer hybrids, they are now considered hardy in the UK. Height varies from 30cm (12in) to 75cm (30in), depending on the species and cultivar. Propagation is by division or seed for new cultivars.

Agastache 'Blue Fortune' (Giant Hyssop)

A clump-forming herbaceous perennial with spikes of violet-blue flowers in the summer and through to the autumn. They grow to a height of 50–75cm (20–30in) and form clumps of 30–45cm (12–18in) in diameter. *Agastache* grow well in most soils, prefer a sunny site and are very useful in dry areas like gravel gardens and herbaceous or mixed borders. The leaves are liquorice-scented.

Agastache foeniculum (Anise Hyssop)

An upright herbaceous perennial with spikes of blue flowers and violet-coloured bracts from midsummer to autumn. It grows to 1m (3¼ft) in height with 60cm (24in) or more spread. The leaves have an aniseed scent.

Agave americana (Century Plant)

A rosette-shaped perennial succulent with very good drought tolerance. It was considered half hardy, but with the effects of climate change is certainly hardy in

Agastache foeniculum.

Agave americana.

the southern UK. The most likely cause of any winter failure will be wet soils rather than cold. The individual leaves can reach 1–1.5m (3¼–5ft) long (even longer in mature plants) and have a sharp point at the end, so be aware of these. Once mature, they will flower on long stems with white bell-shaped flowers, which make quite an impact.

Agave parryi (Parry's Agave)

Another rosette-shaped succulent with grey-green leaves up to 30cm (12in) long, with a dark coloured spike on the end. Again, they were considered to be half hardy but I have seen them growing outdoors over winter in the south of England; if winters become milder, they will be hardy in southern UK. They are

Agastache aurantiaca 'Blue Fortune'.

Agave parryi.

Alchemilla mollis.

worth trying now if they can be protected by fleece during the midwinter period. They are useful in gravel gardens, very dry soils, containers (making them easy to move inside, if required) and Mediterranean gardens.

Ajuga reptans 'Atropurpurea' (Bugle)

An evergreen and very low-growing plant, usually up to 10cm (4in), although it will have a blue flower spike in the spring that may reach 15cm (6in) height. It gives a nice purple colour to the front to a border, which contrasts well with grey foliage. *Ajuga* prefers a shady site and moist soil, so will be useful in the wetter areas of the country and is a useful herbaceous groundcover plant. Propagation is by division and softwood cuttings in the spring.

Alchemilla mollis (Lady's Mantle)

A very tough drought-tolerant plant with greenish-yellow flowers and rounded, soft, pale green leaves

covered in short hairs, both of which are widely used by flower arrangers. It will self-seed and grows in any soil, as well as in sun or shade. After flowering, trim the plant back and it will produce fresh foliage.

Allium (Ornamental Onion)

There are a wide range of *Alliums* available; three are illustrated here.

The colour range of *Alliums* is white through to pink, lilac, purple or blue, depending on the species and cultivar grown. They can be purchased as plants in pots or bulbs, which should be planted to twice their depth in the soil. *Alliums* will tolerate some shade and dry areas. Their height varies depending on the species; the lowest ones approximately 20cm (8in), up to

Ajuga reptans 'Atropurpurea'.

Allium senescens subsp. *Glaucum.*

Allium glaucum 'Globemaster'.

Alstroemeria 'Indian Summer'.

Allium 'Purple Rain'.

Anemone × *hybrida* 'Andrea Atkinson' (Japanese Anemone)

Large white flowers carried on wiry stems up to a height of 1.2m (4ft) in late summer or early autumn. A fairly vigorous plant that will grow in sun or shade. It will tolerate both dry and damp conditions and most soils.

Armeria pseudarmeria (Thrift) and *A. pseudarmeria* 'Dreameria Daydream'

The species has white flowers; the cultivar 'Dreameria Daydream' is available in pink. They are low-growing plants that form a small, rounded clump at first but, if

1m (3¼ft) for the taller species or cultivars. All are hardy and will tolerate dry conditions. Propagation is by seed or dividing the clusters of bulbs.

Alstroemeria 'Indian Summer' (Peruvian Lily)

The older species *Alstroemeria* were nearly 1m (3¼ft) tall, but the newer hybrids are much shorter, up to 45–90cm (18–35in). 'Indian Summer' has brightly coloured flowers of a coppery orange with yellow in them, and dark green to bronze leaves. They have a long flowering period from summer to autumn and will grow in full sun or partial shade in most soils. Propagation is by division in the spring.

Anemone × *hybrida* 'Andrea Atkinson'.

Armeria pseudarmeria 'Dreameria Daydream'.

Artemisia ludoviciana 'Valerie Finnis'.

Armeria pseudarmeria.

left, will grow into each other, forming a larger mat. *Armeria* flower from late spring to summer on stems approximately 15cm (6in) high. If deadheaded they will produce more flowers. The above two plants are taller than the *Armeria maritima* (sea thrift), so will stand out better in borders and are ideal for coastal gardens, gravel gardens, rock gardens, containers and the front of borders.

Artemisia ludoviciana 'Valerie Finnis' (Western Mugwort)

A very attractive herbaceous perennial with grey-white leaves. The plants grow to 75cm (30in) and like well-drained soils in full sun. They are often planted at the front of borders, making a big impact all summer owing to their bright leaves. A good drought-tolerant plant, suitable for gravel gardens, Mediterranean borders and containers.

Aruncus dioicus (Goat's Beard)

A tall herbaceous perennial, up to 2m (6½ft) high, with masses of small white flowers in midsummer; owing to its size it can have a dramatic effect on a border. It is drought tolerant and will grow in partial shade. Once flowering has finished, trim off the dead flowers to tidy the plant, as the foliage still looks attractive.

Aster x *frikartii* 'Mönch' (Michaelmas Daisy)

An *Aster* that does not suffer from powdery mildew; it has lavender-blue daisy-like flowers with yellow centres, typical of many asters. It forms upright clumps, 50–75cm (20–30in) high, which are better given some support or they flop over just as they come into flower.

Aruncus dioicus.

Aster × *frikartii* 'Mönch'.

They flower from late summer to autumn, giving a very good reliable display of colour.

Astilbe 'Bronze Elegans' (False Goat's Beard)

This *Astilbe* has both attractive foliage and flowers, giving a long period of interest. They are summer flowering with panicles of white, pink or red flowers, which if left will turn brown and last into the winter. They need partial shade and a moist soil, so will suit parts of the country that will have a wetter climate in the future as climate change progresses.

Astrantia 'Large White' (Greater Masterwort)

This *Astrantia* has greenish-white flowers surrounded by the same-coloured bracts, which give a long period

Astilbe 'Bronze Elegans'.

Astrantia 'Large White'.

of interest during the summer. They will grow in sun or partial shade, will tolerate clay soils and form clumps up to 50cm (20in) high. Other species of *Astrantia* have red or pink flowers or bracts.

Ballota pseudodictamnus (False Dittany)

An evergreen subshrub with grey-green leaves, owing to being covered by hairs. It is very useful in containers, especially hanging baskets where it will trail down, hiding the pots. It tolerates dry conditions. It looks good with a wide range of bedding plants when used in containers or beds. Propagate by softwood or greenwood cuttings taken to overwinter indoors.

Ballota pseudodictamnus.

Baptisia 'Blue Towers' (Wild Indigo)

Baptisia has violet-blue pea-like flowers in the summer, with light greyish-green foliage and a clump-forming upright habit up to 75cm (30in). It flowers in midsummer and the flowers are followed by inflated seed pods, giving additional interest. It is very drought tolerant and grows well in dry sandy soils in full sun.

Baptisia australis 'Blue Towers'.

Bergenia 'Bizet' (Elephant's Ears)

A large glossy-leaved, evergreen herbaceous perennial with pink flowers in the spring. It will grow in sun or partial shade and in wet or dry sites. Most *Bergenia* are approximately 40–60cm (16–24in) high and will spread slowly to form a good dense groundcover. The size of the leaves add interest to the border and contrast well with smaller leaves.

Brunnera macrophylla 'Jack Frost' (Siberian Bugloss)

Brunnera have large heart-shaped leaves with silvery markings and small blue forget-me-not-like flowers in the spring. It grows very well in shade and will tolerate dry conditions. It can die back a bit in late summer, but compensates for this by coming into leaf early in the spring. It has a height of 45cm (18in) and spreads slowly to 40–50cm (20–25in).

Bergenia 'Bizet'.

Brunnera macrophylla 'Jack Frost'.

Calendula officinalis 'Fiesta' (Pot Marigold)

A colourful annual with orange or yellow flowers (some newer cultivars have cream-coloured flowers); all are available in single or double forms, flowering from early summer to autumn. It will tolerate very dry conditions and is useful in containers as well as dry, sandy soils. It can be sown in either September for early flowering or March or April for summer flowering. The dwarf cultivars grow to 20–30cm (8–12in), so are very useful in containers, and the taller ones reach 50cm (20in). It grows in most soils and will self-seed to continue the display next year.

Campanula poscharskyana (Serbian Bellflower)

A low-growing semi-evergreen herbaceous perennial with lavender-blue, star-shaped flowers. It flowers from summer to autumn, giving a good show of colour.

Calendula 'Fiesta'.

Campanula poscharskyana.

The plant spreads by underground runners and can be invasive and rampant, but is useful on poor soils and where good groundcover is required. The height is only 10cm (4in) and it will spread 50cm (20in) or more. It will grow in sun or shade as well as trailing down walls, as shown in the picture.

Campsis radicans (Trumpet Vine)

A large deciduous climber that will cover a whole wall or half a house, *Campsis* flowers in late summer to early autumn and, if you have space, are worth growing. It grows to 12m (13yd) tall and in late summer produces many orange flowers that are 6–8cm (2½–3¼in) long, which make a good impact. It is native to the southern states of North America and will tolerate the rising temperatures from climate change.

Campsis radicans.

Cerastium tomentosum (Snow-in-Summer)

A good groundcover herbaceous perennial plant that will tolerate hot, dry conditions and poor soils. The foliage is grey-green and the white flowers last from late spring to summer, giving a long period of interest. It grows up to 20–30cm (8–12in) high and can spread up to 1m (3¼ft) – if it becomes too rampant, trim back with shears and it will regrow with no ill effects. Although considered a bit of a thug by some, it is easily contained by annual trimmings and is useful on poor, dry soils.

Cerastium tomentosum.

Ceratostigma willmottianum and *C. plumbaginoides* (Blue Leadwood)

In late summer to autumn, the bright blue flowers on these subshrubs grow to only 45cm (18in), so fit well into small gardens or the front of border locations. Trim them back each spring and they will flower later in the year.

Ceratostigma willmottianum.

Ceratostigma plumbaginoides.

Chamaerops humilis (European Fan Palm)

A slow-growing evergreen dwarf fan palm with leaves that are 60–90cm (24–35in) across and fan-shaped, hence its common name. It is hardy, useful to give a tropical effect to borders and will tolerate hot, dry conditions.

Cortaderia selloana 'Pumila' (Pampas Grass)

A large evergreen grass that is an architectural plant. It makes an impact on borders as it forms solid clumps up to 1.5m (5ft) high. The extensive root system gives it good drought tolerance and it will grow in most soils.

Chamaerops humilis.

Cortaderia selloana 'Pumila'.

The large plumes of flowers are produced in late summer and will last into the winter, unless battered by severe winds.

Crinum × powellii (Swamp Lily)

Crinum is hardy in southern UK and with climate change is likely to be hardy further north. It likes a sunny position in well-drained soil. It flowers in late summer on stems 1m (3¼ft) or more tall with large, pink, funnel-shaped flowers. The leaves are straplike and semi-evergreen, especially in mild winters or areas. It grows well in gravel gardens and containers or other free-draining sites. A white-flowered cultivar is also available.

Crocosmia 'Lucifer' (Montbretia)

This grows from a corm and can form large clumps of upright sword-shaped leaves, contrasting well with other plants with rounded leaves. 'Lucifer' has bright red flowers in summer to autumn, although there are other cultivars with orange or yellow flowers. The heights

Crinum × powellii 'Album'.

Crocosmia 'Lucifer'.

vary, depending on the species or cultivar, from 40cm (16in) to 1m (3¼ft). It is reliable and grows in most soils.

Dianella caerulea (Blue Flax Lily)

This has dark green, straplike evergreen leaves and was not considered fully hardy but now grows in a number of gardens in southern UK, without any winter protection. It is likely to be hardy further north as climate change progresses. It grows to a height of 50–75cm (20–30in) with small blue flowers, but its main attraction are the bright blue berries that follow; the colour adds an extra dimension to the palate. Grown in sun or light shade, it is suitable for most soils.

Dichondra argentea 'Silver Falls' (Silver Nickel Vine)

A slightly tender herbaceous perennial with evergreen silver-white leaves. It may survive outdoors in

Dianella caerulea.

Dichondra argentea 'Silver Falls'.

sheltered mild areas, especially as climate change progresses. It is used in hanging baskets and containers, trailing down the sides, where the growth can be up to 1m (3¼ft) in length. It grows in full sun or partial shade and is drought tolerant. A very useful summer bedding plant that may overwinter in parts of the country.

Digitalis purpurea (Foxglove)

The native Foxglove, which grows well in semi-shade, is normally grown as a biennial but will occasionally survive as a short-lived perennial. The species has pink-purple flowers, hence its species name, but it is available in white and now in some other colours. Foxgloves will grow up to 1.5m (5ft) tall, although some of the newer cultivars are smaller. Bees are frequent visitors to the flowers, which open up the stem in late spring to early summer. A very colourful plant and, although the leaves often wilt, the plants will survive dry conditions.

Echeveria elegans (Mexican Snowball)

A rosette-shaped perennial succulent with silvery leaves that will produce red/yellow flowers in the summer. It is hardy in southern UK and, as the effects of climate change evolve, will be hardy further north. It is very drought-tolerant but needs a free-draining soil over winter to avoid root rot. *Echeveria* grows well in containers, gravel gardens, roof gardens and at the front of borders, giving a tropical effect.

Echinacea purpurea (Purple Coneflower)

A herbaceous perennial from North America that grows in both wet and dry habitats on the prairies. It

Echeveria elegans.

Digitalis purpurea mixed.

Echinacea purpurea 'Magnus'.

Echinacea purpurea 'Sensation Pink'.

has purple flowers from midsummer to autumn. There are now cultivars with white or yellow flowers, although these are not as vigorous as the species. It is well worth considering for herbaceous and mixed borders and will grow in grass, as long as it is not too dense.

Echinops bannaticus 'Taplow Blue' (Small Globe Thistle)

A reliable perennial with blue flowers that dry well for use indoors. It has a long flowering period during the summer. It will grow in most soils, up to a height of 1.5m (5ft), although there are taller and shorter species and cultivars. It is drought tolerant and can spread a little if allowed to self-seed.

Echinops bannaticus 'Taplow Blue'.

Eryngium giganteum (Miss Willmott's Ghost)

This species is a biennial or short-lived perennial that usually dies after flowering but is still worth growing. It can reach a height of 75cm (30in) to 1m (3¼ft) and sometimes taller. The lower leaves are green with white veins and the flowers are blue, surrounded by silvery coloured bracts, which give the plant a dramatic effect. Flowering occurs in late summer and the bracts will last into the winter. Other species of Eryngium are perennial and most are smaller; *Eryngium × zabelii* 'Blue Waves' is worth a look.

Eryngium × zabelii 'Blue Waves' (Sea Holly)

A hybrid from Hilliers nursery in Hampshire, which will grow in poor soils and is drought tolerant. The leaves have silver veining and the flowers are blue, surrounded with blue bracts, which again can be left into the winter for added interest. It gives its best

Eryngium 'Miss Willmott's Ghost'.

Eryngium × zabelii 'Blue Waves'.

colour in poor, free-draining soils, and climate change should suit it.

Eschscholzia californica (California Poppy)

These are now available with red, yellow or orange flowers, which give colour over a long period, growing to a height of 30–45cm (12–18in). They have grey-green feathery foliage, which gives added interest and helps to give the plants drought tolerance. Their native habitat are the deserts of California so they are well used to dry and drought conditions. *Eschscholzia* is hardy in the UK, despite being from California. It can be sown in September outdoors and will overwinter, flowering in late spring. It can also be sown in March or

April for summer flowering and will self-seed. A very useful plant for sunny and dry sites.

Euonymus fortunei 'Emerald 'n' Gold' (Evergreen Bittersweet)

A common and useful evergreen shrub that will grow in most soils in sun or partial shade. It is widely used commercially in landscape plantings but is still worth considering for garden use. It grows to a height of 1–1.5m (3¼–5ft) but can be trimmed to keep it lower, if required. If planted adjacent to a wall, it will lean against it to use it for support and can grow up to 2m (6½ft) in height. The leaves are a green and gold variegation, which look particularly bright in the spring. It will grow in dry conditions and will tolerate wet soils in the winter.

Fritillaria imperialis (Crown Imperial)

A tall, majestic plant that gives a good show of colour in the spring and then dies down before the really dry

Eschscholzia californica.

Euonymus fortunei 'Emerald 'n' Gold'.

Fritillaria imperialis yellow.

Galtonia candicans.

Fritillaria imperialis orange.

Geraniums

These are low-growing carpeting plants with masses of flowers during the summer. Some are early summer flowering; others start later and go through to the autumn. They will grow in sun or shade in most soil conditions and are drought-tolerant. They have semi-evergreen foliage, which can be trimmed back if it starts to get untidy.

Geranium 'Rozanne' won 'Chelsea Plant of the Centenary' for the decade 1993–2002 and was the winner of the public vote. It has violet-blue flowers with a whiteish centre, flowers over a long period and grows in most soils in sun or partial shade. A plant to be recommended, as it is very reliable and tolerates dry conditions.

weather occurs, avoiding the summer droughts. It is available with yellow or orange flowers, which are held on top of 1m- (3¼ft-) high stems. It is native from Turkey through to Afghanistan, so is well used to hot, dry conditions. The foliage smell can be a bit off-putting to some people.

Galtonia candicans (Summer Hyacinth)

A summer-flowering bulb that can grow to nearly 1m (3¼ft) tall in the right conditions. It has straplike leaves of a grey-green colour and stems with funnel-shaped white flowers. *Galtonia* are better planted in a sheltered sunny position but will tolerate some shade. They do not like dry conditions.

Geranium (Rozanne) 'Gerwat'.

Geranium 'Orion'.

Gypsophila paniculata 'Compacta Plena' (Baby's Breath)

This grows to 75cm (30in) with frothy white flowers on wiry stems in the summer. The small leaves are grey-green and the plant has a delicate appearance. The root system is quite large, giving it a good tolerance to drought.

Hedera helix and H. colchica (Ivy)

Ivies are very good evergreen climbers that can also be used for ground covering. There is a wide range of green or variegated cultivars, which will grow in most soils and in sun or shade. They have a wide range of leaf sizes, and some are more vigorous than others, so choose one to suit your circumstances. They will hide unsightly walls or other constructions and provide a very good habitat for insects and birds.

Hedera helix 'Goldchild'.

Gypsophila paniculata 'Compacta Plena'.

Hedera colchica 'Sulphur Heart'.

Helenium 'Moerheim Beauty' (Sneezeweed)

These have daisy-like flowers with reddish-orange petals and a dark brown centre in late summer. They are very reliable flowerers and grow in most soils. There are other species and cultivars with a wider colour range, including yellow. They give a reliable flower display, even in hot conditions.

Helichrysum petiolare.

Helenium 'Moerheim Beauty'.

Helichrysum petiolare (Licorice Plant)

A small evergreen subshrub that looks more like a herbaceous plant and is often used in hanging baskets, containers and bedding displays as an annual plant. The leaves and stems are silver-grey-green with a felted appearance, making it very tolerant to dry conditions. It is not fully hardy but can be overwintered in a cool greenhouse, and is easily propagated by softwood cuttings.

Hemerocallis 'Lilioasphodelus' and *H.* 'Stafford' (Day Lily)

This is a yellow-flowered day lily, but they are available in a wide range of colours and heights. They will grow in most soils, as long as it is not too wet, and flower better in a sunny position. Although each

Hemerocallis lilioasphodelus.

flower only opens for a day, the plant will continue to flower for four to six weeks once established. *Hemerocallis* 'Stafford' shows a darker-coloured and larger flower, illustrating the range of colours available.

Hemerocallis 'Stafford'.

Iris pallida 'Argentea Variegata'.

Hydrangea viburnoides (Climbing Hydrangea)

This used to be called *Pileostegia* and before that *Schizophragma viburnoides,* and it is still sold under those names. They are attractive climbers that will cling to walls or fences and display clusters of small white flowers from summer to autumn. They grow to 6m (6½yd) in sun or shade, including on north-facing walls, giving much needed colour to often dull sites.

Iris pallida 'Argentea Variegata' (Sweet Iris)

A rhizomatous Iris that has attractive variegated foliage and in late spring has lilac-blue flowers, typical of 'Bearded Iris'. It will tolerate dry and damp conditions and gives a long display of interest. The spiky foliage contrasts well with rounded and clump-forming plants.

Iris pseudacorus (Yellow Iris)

The native yellow flag Iris, which will grow in both water and wet areas so will be useful on clay soils that could sit wet over winter, owing to the increased rainfall predicted. It can spread, so may need some plants removing occasionally.

Hydrangea viburnoides.

Iris pseudacorus.

Kniphofia 'Bees' Lemon' (Red-hot Poker)

Kniphofia have an erect habit with spikes of flower in late summer to autumn. The colours range from yellow through to oranges and reds. They are now considered hardy in the UK, but if concerned, mulching around the plants will protect them from frosts. The foliage is evergreen in most species.

Lagerstroemia indica (Crepe Myrtle)

A deciduous small tree or large shrub that has masses of pink or white flowers in summer to early autumn. It is hardy in southern UK and is worth trying in the Midlands and further north in sheltered areas for its summer flowering.

Kniphofia 'Bees' Lemon'.

Lagerstroemia indica.

Liatris spicata 'Kobold' (Button Snakewort)

This has straplike leaves with pink-purple flowers in late summer, which tend to stand out in the border, despite being only 30–40cm (12–16in) in height. It is a good front-of-border plant and is well worth considering.

Limnanthes douglasii (Poached Egg Plant)

An early flowering annual with light green feathery foliage and yellow and white flowers, looking a bit like a poached egg, hence its common name 'poached

Liatris spicata 'Kobold'.

Limnanthes douglasii.

egg plant'. If sown or allowed to self-sow in the autumn, it will flower in late spring; if sown in the spring, it flowers in the summer. *Limnanthes* are low-growing – only about 10–15cm (4–6in) high – and produce plenty of colour. It grows in most soils (including gravel) in sun and partial shade. The one disadvantage is that once it has flowered it dies back, leaving a gap in the display, so it can pay to have a few plants ready to fill these.

Limonium platyphyllum (Sea Lavender)

Previously called *Limonium latifolium*, this forms clumps of leaves in sunny sites and dry conditions. It has large, leathery dark green leaves with frothy blue flowers in late summer, which are useful for drying for indoor flower displays.

Lobelia cardinalis 'Queen Victoria' (Cardinal Flower)

This cultivar has purple foliage with bright red flowers from late summer. It has an upright habit – up to 1m (3¼ft) in height – and will give definition to a border. It

Lobelia cardinalis 'Queen Victoria'.

will grow in wet and boggy conditions but can often be attacked by slugs, which also like similar conditions. There are other *Lobelia cardinalis* cultivars with white or pink flowers and purple foliage, and also with red, white and pink flowers and green foliage.

Lupinus 'Beefeater' (Lupins)

Lupins are available in a range of bright colours that flower in early summer, with pea-like flowers on upright stems. They are one of the earlier herbaceous

Limonium platyphyllum.

Lupinus spp..

Lupinus arcticus 'Beefeater'.

plants to flower and can make a good impact. The plants form clumps of attractive foliage with flower spikes of up to 1.2m (4ft). Once the flowers have gone over, remove the stem to tidy the plant.

Melianthus major (Great Honey Flower)

An evergreen shrub that is considered half hardy but grows outdoors in southern UK and will grow further north as the climate warms. The leaves are fairly large,

Melianthus major.

being 25–40cm (10–16in) long, with bluish-grey leaflets. It will grow in dry conditions, although it may need water in severe droughts, but it is worth a try. *Melianthus* are grown for their foliage and are often used to create a tropical effect in borders.

Miscanthus sinensis (Chinese Silver Grass)

A clump-forming perennial grass that is nearly evergreen as it retains its old foliage overwinter. The seedheads also give winter interest, especially when

Miscanthus sinensis 'China'.

Miscanthus sinensis 'Morning Light'.

rimed in frost. *Miscanthus* will give a bit of structure to the garden when most herbaceous plants have died down. It produces flower spikes in the autumn, which give further interest. Their height can vary depending on the cultivar, as can the leaf colour – some being plain green but others being variegated.

Musa basjoo (Banana)

Commonly called the Japanese banana, it has a tropical appearance with its large leaves that will grow up to 1m (3¼ft) in length, as well as producing green fruit some years. It is not fully hardy in the UK, but with climate change it will survive outdoors if well wrapped with straw or fleece. As the climate warms, this protection may not be required in the future.

Muscari armeniacum (Grape Hyacinth)

This produces blue flowers in the spring, giving a good show of early low-growing colour. It is easy to grow in

Muscari armeniacum.

most soils and dies down through the summer, so avoids the droughts. *Muscari* grows to a height of 15–20cm (6–8in) and can self-seed. It is also available with white flowers.

Narcissus Species and Cultivars (Daffodil)

Many narcissi are native to Europe. As they grow over winter, flower in the spring and then die down by early summer, they usually miss the worse effects of droughts. There are a number of species available with numerous cultivars – and more being bred each year! The colour range is from white through yellow to orange and nearly red, and heights vary from 15–50cm

Musa basjoo.

Narcissus 'Tahiti'.

Narcissus 'White Lion'.

(6–20in). Narcissus is a very useful spring flowering bulb, giving good displays of colour each spring.

Nigella damascena (Love-in-a-Mist)

A very useful annual with attractive feathery foliage with blue or white flowers, followed by small balloon-like seedheads, which can be dried. It will self-seed and create a swathe of late spring colour the next year, even in gravel gardens. *Nigella* can be sown in September for early flowers the next year or in March or April for summer flowering. There are dwarf

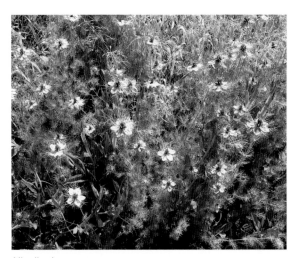

Nigella damascena.

cultivars growing to a height of 30cm (12in) and taller types that are nearly 60cm (24in).

Opuntia ficus-indica (Prickly Pear)

The edible prickly pear is a cactus that is hardy in southern regions and will give a desert-like appearance to gravel gardens and borders. It produces masses of yellow flowers in the summer, which are followed by the edible purple fruits.

Opuntia ficus-indica.

Parthenocissus tricuspidata (Boston Ivy)

A deciduous climbing shrub with an excellent autumn crimson colour. It is a vigorous plant that will cover a large area of wall or fence, up to 15m (16yd) high, and is self-clinging so is very useful for covering large unsightly walls, especially on the ends of buildings.

Parthenocissus tricuspidata 'Fenway Park'.

Punica granatum 'Hazel Hyde'.

Phlomis russeliana (Turkish Sage)

An evergreen perennial with large grey-green leaves and yellow flowers in mid to late summer. The seed-heads last well into the winter to give added interest. It is a good groundcover plant that can be a bit rampant, but is easily cut back or dug out. It tolerates dry conditions and grows in both sun and partial shade. The leaves grow to approximately 30cm (12in) in height and the flower stems to 75cm (30in) to 100cm (3½ft).

Punica granatum (Pomegranate)

A small- to medium-sized shrub with red flowers followed by edible orange-red fruits. It used to be

Punica granatum 'Hazel Hyde', close up.

considered tender but will definitely grow outdoors all the year round in southern UK, especially if in a sheltered position. *Punica* has small glossy green deciduous leaves and grows to 1.5–2m (5–6½ft) high. Originating from Mediterranean areas, it is used to dry summers.

Rudbeckia fulgida var. *deamii* (Coneflower)

Another late-summer flowering perennial with daisy-like yellow flowers that is useful in prairie planting or in large borders, giving good blocks of colour. The petals are bright yellow with a brown cone in the centre. It grows to a height of 75cm (30in) and will spread slowly to 1m (3¼ft) or so but is not rampant. Flowers better in a sunny site.

Phlomis russeliana.

Rudbeckia fulgida var. deamii.

Rudbeckia fulgida var. sullivantii 'Goldsturm'.

Santolina chamaecyparissus (Cotton Lavender)

A typical Mediterranean shrub with grey-white leaves and bright yellow flowers in mid to late summer. It grows to 50cm (20in) with a spread of 75cm (30in) to 1m (3¼ft) but can be trimmed to be kept smaller, if required. They are suitable for dwarf hedges around knot gardens or other internal hedges. Being a

Santolina incana.

Mediterranean native, they are drought tolerant and have a long period of interest.

Sedum album 'Coral Carpet' (Stonecrop)

This *Sedum* has white flowers with red tinted foliage. It grows to a height of 10cm (4in) and forms clumps up to 15cm (6in) in size. It is useful in containers, gravel, roof gardens and on free-draining soils. It flowers in mid-summer, which contrasts very nicely with its red leaves.

Sedum kamtschaticum var. *floriferum* 'Weihenstephaner Gold'

A semi-evergreen low-growing (10cm/4in) *Sedum* with dark green leaves and bright yellow flowers in the

Sedum album 'Coral Carpet'.

Sedum kamtschaticum var. *floriferum* 'Weihenstephaner Gold'.

summer. The seedheads last into the autumn, when the leaves also turn reddish-purple, giving the plant a long period of interest. Being drought tolerant, they are useful on roof gardens.

Sedum 'Matrona'

Also known as *Hylotelephium* 'Matrona', this is an upright clump-forming herbaceous perennial with succulent grey-green leaves that are tinged with purple. The plant is topped off with clusters of pink flowers in summer to early autumn. 'Matrona' grows to approximately 60cm (24in) and is very drought tolerant, useful in gravel gardens, coastal gardens and fronts of borders.

Sedum 'Red Cauli'

Also known as *Hylotelephium* 'Red Cauli', this is a very colourful clump-forming herbaceous perennial with dark pink flowers in late summer, which can be left for winter interest. It grows to 30cm (12in) high with a spread of 50cm (20in). The foliage is dark green to blue-green and succulent, making it very drought tolerant, and it can be grown in full sun or light shade.

Sedum 'Red Cauli'.

Sempervivum (Houseleek)

A range of species showing the diverse nature and colour of the *Sempervivum* genus.

Sedum 'Matrona'.

Sempervivums.

Sempervivum calcareum

An evergreen mat-forming plant with grey-green leaves in rosettes up to 20cm (8in) in diameter and pinkish flowers in the summer. Very drought tolerant and useful in containers, especially if watering is inconsistent, although it will not tolerate wet or waterlogged conditions.

Senecio candidans 'Angel Wings' (Shining White Ragwort)

An evergreen perennial with large silver-white leaves, used in bedding schemes and containers during the summer. It is hardy in sheltered mild areas, especially if grown in containers and moved adjacent to a wall for protection from the worst of the weather. With the warming climate it will be worth leaving outside in the southern UK.

Senecio cineraria 'Silver Dust' (Silver Ragwort)

Usually grown as an annual and used in containers and bedding schemes, this is actually a short-lived perennial. It can be killed by severe frost but survives in my garden most years; it looks a bit of a mess by the spring but, if trimmed back, soon produces fresh attractive silver foliage. During the summer it will produce bright yellow daisy-like flowers, which should be removed once they have gone over. It will grow in full sun or partial shade and owing to its grey leaves has good drought tolerance.

Sisyrinchium striatum (Yellow-eyed Grass)

A semi-evergreen plant with leaves that look like the 'Flag Iris', being straight and upright with a narrow-pointed end and grey-green in colour. The flowers are small and light yellow during the summer.

Sempervivum calcareum.

Senecio candidans 'Angel Wings'.

Senecio cineraria 'Silver Dust'.

Sisyrinchium striatum.

Solanum crispum 'Glasnevin'.

Solanum crispum 'Glasnevin' (Dublin) (Chilean Potato Tree)

An evergreen shrub with a scrambling habit of growth, so it needs some support like a trellis to keep it upright. It produces potato-like purple-lilac flowers over a long period in the summer, hence its name 'potato tree'; it is in the same genus as the potato. This cultivar was bred in Ireland.

Stachys byzantina (Lamb's Ears)

This has evergreen, hairy grey leaves that form a carpet over the soil. Owing to the colour and hairs, the plants are very drought tolerant. During the summer it

Solanum crispum 'Glasnevin'.

Stachys byzantina 'Big Ears'.

produces pink flowers to give some added interest; once these have gone over, trim back the plants and they will produce fresh foliage. *Stachys* forms a good groundcover in sun or partial shade and is a useful front-of-border plant.

Stipa gigantea (Golden Oats)

An evergreen perennial grass with panicles of flowers in the summer that will last well into the winter, giving good winter interest. It grows up to 2m (6½ft) high so is a plant that can have impact in a border. Owing to its extensive root system, it is fairly drought tolerant.

Trachelospermum jasminoides (Star Jasmine)

An evergreen shrub with twining stems that produce scented, white flowers during the summer. It prefers a sunny position but will tolerate partial shade and grows to a height of 2m (6½ft). Well worth growing for its

Stipa tenuissima.

scent, it will cover an unsightly wall or fence, especially if south facing.

Tulipa Species and Cultivars (Tulip)

Many of the tulip species originate from the Middle East, so are well adapted to dry summers when they have died down to underground. They produce foliage over winter, flower in the spring and die back by early summer, before the really hot dry conditions start. They give an excellent show of colour over the spring period with a wide range of colours available. Height can vary from 15cm (6in) to 50cm (20in), depending on the species and cultivars being grown. Tulips do not like wet conditions over winter, so are better grown in containers if your soil is a heavy clay.

Stipa gigantea 'Gold Fontaene'.

Tulipa 'Bright Flair'.

Tulipa 'Crystal Beauty'.

Ulex europaeus 'Flore Pleno' (Gorse)

This produces bright yellow long-lasting flowers in mid-spring, when peak flowering occurs, and then on and off during the summer through to the autumn. It grows well on poor soils and is very drought resistant, forming a mound of very spiny green branches.

Ulex europaeus 'Flore Pleno'.

Ulex europaeus 'Flore Pleno'.

Verbascum bombyciferum 'Arctic Summer' (Mullein)

A biennial or a short-lived perennial; in year one the plant produces a large rosette of silver-grey leaves that look attractive over winter and early spring, then during

Verbascum 'Arctic Summer'.

the next summer it grows a tall – up to 2m (6½ft) high – flower spike with yellow flowers in the summer. Grown in full sun, they give better leaf colour in poor soils. It is drought tolerant and makes a good impact in the borders.

Verbena bonariensis (Purple Top Vervain)

A plant that has been fashionable for a number of years now; it is useful to give height to beds and borders without blocking the view of what is behind. It produces small purplish flowers on wiry stems in late summer to autumn and will self-seed, if allowed. A good plant for pollinating insects that will grow in most soils – even poor, dry types – and gravel gardens.

Verbena rigida (Slender Vervain)

A lower-growing plant, similar to *Verbena bonariensis*, with violet flowers on stems up to 45cm (18in) height in midsummer, which again are good for pollinating insects and grow in most soils.

Verbena rigida.

Veronicastrum virginicum 'Lavendelturm' (Culvers Root)

A tall upright herbaceous perennial with masses of flowers down the stem in late summer. There are several cultivars available with a colour range of white to pink. It is a very useful plant to give height to herbaceous and mixed borders.

Verbena bonariensis.

Veronicastrum virginicum 'Lavendelturm'.

Vinca minor 'Bowles Variety' (Periwinkle)

An evergreen dwarf spreading shrub, usually no more than 20cm (8in) high, that grows in dense mats so is very useful for groundcover, even in dense shade (the variegated forms are better grown in good light). There are both dark green-leaved and variegated types available and flower colours can be blue, white or purple flowering in the spring. They will grow in most soils and have a reasonable drought tolerance, especially if grown in shade.

Yucca filamentosa (Adam's Needle)

An evergreen woody-stemmed plant that can be single stemmed or produce a number of stems from the base of the plant. Despite its looks, it is fully hardy and will produce large white flowers in the summer on a long stem. The leaves are sword-shaped with a sharp spike on the end. The plant adds an architectural effect to borders and fits in well to gravel gardens, Mediterranean gardens and containers. It is very drought tolerant and grows well in full sun or partial shade.

Vinca minor 'Bowles' Variety'.

Zauschneria californica 'Dublin' (California fuchsia)

A subshrub of approximately 30–40cm (12–16in) high with orange-scarlet flowers in midsummer to autumn. It gives a colourful display for the front of borders and looks good trailing down stone walls. Another plant from California, so it is well used to dry and drought conditions. It will not tolerate wet soils so may need some protection if winters are too wet. It can be propagated by softwood cuttings so could be over-wintered indoors if need be, or grown in containers and moved to a sheltered dry position overwinter. It prefers a sunny site to give maximum colour.

Yucca filamentosa flowers.

Zauschneria californica 'Dublin'.

INDEX